Management of Occupational Stress

Management of Occupational Stress

Theories and Practice

A.K. Srivastava

GYAN

Published by

GYAN

Gyan Publishing House
5, Ansari Road
Daryaganj, New Delhi-110002
Phone: 011-47034999, 9811692060
E-mail: books@gyanbooks.com

Distribution Network
gyanbooks.com
India, USA, Canada, UK, Australia, France

ISBN: 978-81-212-0666-2 (HB)

Reprint in India, 2024
First Published, 1999

Printed at: Gyan Press, Delhi.

Management of Occupational Stress: Theory and Practice
Author: A.K. Srivastava

CONTENTS

PREFACE

In contemporary societies majority of people seem to talking about stress and its various consequences. Individual's reactions to severe stress has become the major concern of the stress researchers in different disciplines, such as psychology, psychiatry, medical sciences, physiology and management. An ever increasing number of books and journals devoted to stress are coming up and various courses and seminars on stress are being organized all over world. Substantial amount of research has been done by stress researchers of different disciplines to reveal the causes and consequences of psychological stress. These researches have established that high and consistent stress is unpleasant and undesirable, and leads to a variety of psychological and somatic pathologies. Consistently increasing rate of psychosomatic diseases and psychological disorders in modern societies well reflect the high stress being experienced by people in present day world.

Job life, wherein, employees spend about more than one third of their daily routine is the major source of satisfaction of their various needs, as well as of frustration and stress. Occupational stress has been noted to put impairing effect on employees job behaviour and physical and psychological well being, representing serious cost to organizations in human and monetary terms. After having recognized Seriousness of the consequencest of occupational stress, the stress researchers and concerned professionals have now concentrated on evolving systematic strategies for prevention, mitigation and management of stresses of job life. This volume is also an attempt in this pursuit. The book elaborates various techniques evolved for prevention and management of occupational stress, and provides guidelines to make effective use of these strategies and interventions. Elaboration of various stress management techniques has also been substantiated with related theoretical concepts and relevant researches. Besides the stress management strategies and interventions, the volume comprises separate, though brief, chapters on the concept sources and consequences of occupational stress in the interest of general readers. The volume would prove to be of a great use for those who are concerned with stress management as well as for the employees in managing the stress is of their job life at their own level. It should also be useful as a reference book for stress researchers and general readers.

I am indebted to the sources, particularly the books on stress and stress management written by Goldberger and Brenzwit (1982), Lehrer and Woolfolk (1993), and Ross and Altmaier (1994), which have been of immense help in the preparation of this volume. There are many people whom I wish to thank for their physical, psychological, or social support in completion of this volume. First of all, I would like to express my sincere gratitude to my teacher, Professor D.M. Pestonjee, who has always been a great source of inspiration and enabled me to reach this level. I am thankful also to my colleagues who motivated me and extended academic support to take up this project. Last, but not the least, I wish to thank my wife and children for patiently coping with the experience of stress of a preoccupied husband and father. Finally, I express my gratitude to the Almighty for all I have been able to accomplish.

A. K. Srivastava

1
CONCEPTUAL PERSPECTIVE

Stress

Stress and anxiety have become pervading features of people's life in modern world. Despite tremendous advancements in science and technology, and remarkable growth of economy and sources of luxury, majority of people all over the world seem to be experiencing moderate to high degree of psychological stress in various spheres of their lives. Consistently increasing rate of psychosomatic and psychological disorders, and feeling of frustration and dissatisfaction with life in general reflect the high stress being experienced by the people in the present day world. Not that people in societies in the past were entirely free from stress. People must have been experiencing stress right since the origin of structured societies. However, the causes of stress in those societies were episodic in nature, and low in severity and frequency. But during last two decades frequency, severity and span of psycho-social stress have drastically increased. The basic reason being the tremendously changed physical and socio-cultural environment of the contemporary societies, and lifestyle of the people. People's life in contemporary societies has become more diversely demanding, complicated, mechanical and dependent, and is running by the clock. Ever increasing needs and aspirations, high competition, pressures of meeting dead lines and uncertainty of future and weakened social support system have made the life of majority of people highly stressful in modern societies. This is the reason, the term stress and research in its causes, consequences, and management, have reached the peak of popularity in recent times. The reactions to intense psychological stress has become a major concern of psychological, psychiatric, and medical investigations. However, potential of the term stress as a prime intellectual tool for understanding and explaining individual's behaviour and pathologies has yet not been fully realized by the stress researchers.

In the present day world, majority of people may be seen talking about the term yet, significantly few people use the term in the same way or even attempt for a clear-cut definition of the term stress. The term has been so loosely defined that there have been recommendations that the use of the term be abandoned altogether. Selye (1980) has accordingly stated that "the concept of stress is still fraught with definitional contradictions, and suffers from the mixed blessing of being too well known and too little understood." Ivancevich & Matteson (1980) have even compared stress with sin, as both are considered important by many people even though different people are not always talking about the same thing when they use the word. What has hampered the adequate use of the concept of stress is the fact that different investigators have employed somewhat different referents and meanings for the term stress, and thus have employed different explicit and implicit models.

The term stress has been derived from the Latin word *stringere* which means to draw tight. The term was used to refer to hardship, strain, adversity or affliction. Various terms have been synonymously used with stress, viz., anxiety, frustration, conflict, pressure, strain, etc. The physiologist, Walter Connon (1914), in his work on homeostasis had used the term stress to describe emotional states that had possible detrimental physical impact on the focal organism. In 1935, Cannon modified the use of the term stress to describe physical stimuli and used the term strain for organism's response to the stressor. Some have described the term stress as the quality of stimulus (Dunbar, 1947), while others defined it as the quality of both stimulus and the response. Wolff (1950) described it as a state of human organism. Some others have described it as that class of stimuli which produce anxiety and reportable experience of tense dread (Basowitz, Persky, Korchin, Grinker, 1958). The Concise Oxford Dictionary defines stress in five different ways. But three of these definitions are relevant in present context. The first definition offered is that of a constraining or impelling force (e.g. under the stress examination or poverty). The second definition treats stress as an effect or demand an energy (e.g. subjected to great stress). The third definition talks of a force exerted on the body. In Penguin Medical Encyclopaedia (Wingate, 1972) stress has been described "as any influence which disturbs the natural equilibrium of the body, and includes within its reference, physical injury, exposure, deprivation, all kinds of disease and emotional disturbance". These dictionary definitions of stress may be presented in a model which denote stress as a constraining force acting on a person, who in attempting to cope with this force exerts himself, and consequently feels fatigued or distressed. However, the concept of stress seems to have had special place in the mind of laymen and scientists ever since Selye (1956) popularized the term in his writings on "General Adaptation Syndrome (GAS)." He defined stress as "non-specific responses of the body to any demand made upon it." He was of the opinion that organism makes a universal pattern to response to all types of internal or external demands made on the body. The GAS has three stages, i.e., alarm, resistance, and collapse. The alarm stage is the body's initial response to stressor, e.g., increase heart rate and blood pressure, and release of glucose to provide energy for action. If the stress is prolonged, the stage of resistance emerges. The process of homeostasis comes into play at this stage. The body tries to maintain equilibrium. There is continuing effort to adapt to the stressor during this stage. The body cannot go on coping with stress indefinitely. The third stage of collapse is characterized by a loss of resistance to the stressor, and exhaustion, collapse and even death can occur. But this model of GAS has been challenged by the stress researchers as it does not give any significance to cognitive processes and individual differences in these physical responses to stressors.

There is a wide variation in biological, medical and psychological literature in the definition and use of the term stress. It has been used at times as a stimulus as external negative force impinging upon an individual; as emotional and/or physiological response to internal or external environmental events; and as a state resulted from interaction between individual and his surroundings– a person-environment misfit resulted from perception and appraisal of one's internal or external environments.

Stimulus Perspective of Stress

Stress conceived as a stimulus has been used to describe environmental situations or conditions characterized as new, intense, rapidly changing, demanding, sudden, or unexpected (Beehr, 1984; Beehr & Bhagat, 1985; McLean, 1979; Selye, 1975). Stressful stimuli can also include stimulus deficit, absence of expected stimulation, highly persistent stimulation, fatigue or boredom. In this perspective, stress has been treated as an independent variable. This model of stress is an engineering one in which external stressor gives rise to stress reaction, or strain within the individual (Cox, 1978). Lazarus (1966) also considered such events as failure or the threat of failure, noxious or unpleasant agents in the environment, isolation, and rapid social changes as stress stimuli. Other stimulus situations mentioned in the literature as stressful are (i) losses of personal, physical, cognitive, or affective functions; (ii) frustration of anticipated reward or goal attainment; (iii) failure or change in social feedback mechanism; (iv) impulse flooding; and (v) approach-avoidance conflict situations. Symonds (1947) has also described stress as environmental stimulus. He has written, "it should be understood once and for all that stress is that which happens to the man, not that which happens in-time; it is a set of causes, not a set of symptoms."

The stress as stimulus has triggered active research on relationship between stress and somatic illness. Meyer (1958) long back argued that certain alterations of life circumstances have potential influence on balance between health and illness. Holmes (1974), Rahe (1968) and their collaborators examined in a series of studies whether changes in the life of a person statistically correlate with illness. Studies conducted by Holmes and Rahe (1967) generated a hierarchical list of life event changes likely to require significant alterations in the ongoing adaptive patterns of the individual. The crucial life events are not the direct cause of illness. The important factor which causes illness is the new demand on the usual adaptive patterns of the person. The greater the demand of a social situation or event, for making new adaptive efforts to readjust to it, more is the likelihood that an inadequate response will be that an utilized, thus, eliciting pathological physiological reactions. These social situations or events which require the focal person to make excessive adaptive effort, have been considered as stress, by this group of stress researchers.

But the question arises that which conditions can be accepted as stressful and, what are their common characteristics? Probably the common features of stressful stimuli are undesirable, unpleasant, uncomfortable, threatening, and demanding. Weitz (1970) enlisted eight types of stressful situations, namely speeded information processing, noxious environmental stimuli, perceived threat, disrupted psychological function, isolation, confinement, blocking, group pressures, and frustration. Lazarus (1966) considered perceived threat as the central characteristic of stressful situation. Frankenhaeuser (1975a) has denoted "lack of control over events" as stressful situation.

Thus, we see that all undesirable and excessively demanding stimuli or situations have been considered as stress. But in fact, these stimulus situations may be more suitably called "stressors" instead of "stress." These situations are very likely to cause or generate the feeling of stress in most of the focal persons, but not necessarily in everyone. It is quite difficult to generalize that certain kinds of situations are inherently stressful and certain others are not. People react to their life situations or social conditions in terms of their own interpretative meanings of these situations or events. Much depends upon context, mood, and experience when people come to interpret the meaning of an event. The actual amount of stress-felt is determined by the stressful situations in combination with other personal and situational variables.

Response Perspective of Stress

We all know that "things are seldom what they seem". With exception of extreme and sudden life threatening situations, no raw stimulus is a universal stressor. In this perspective, it is the way in which the individual handles the perceived stressors—the defences it mobilizes and the alarm reactions ignited—that constitutes the true nature of the stress. The emphasis in this perspective is on the meaning of the stimulus, rather than objective nature of the stimulus itself. Theorists who define stress from a response perspective see it as an imbalance between the requirements to make an adaptive response and the repertoire of the focal person. The greater the perceived discrepancy between demand and response capacity and the higher the appraised cost of making such reactions, the more stress there will be impinging on the individual. The term stress has been used to refer to the response to stressor by Beehr (1984), Caplan, Cobb, French, Harrison and Pinneau (1975), and Kahn and Quinn (1970). The response based definition of stress concerns with the specification of the particular response or response patterns which may be taken as evidence that the person is, or has been, under pressure from a 'disturbing' environment. That response or pattern of response is treated as stress or as its defining parameter (Cox, 1978).

There may be something excessive or unusual about a reaction that produces psychological or physiological consequences detrimental to the organism. The presence of emotional activity has been used as a post facto index to determine the existence of stress. From this perspective, stress would be regarded as the demands placed upon the individual to respond adaptively to a stimulus appraised as noxious. Theorists who define stress from a response perspective see it as an 'imbalance' between the requirements to make an adaptive response and the 'repertoire' of the individual. The greater the fraction of expectancies in a situation, and the greater the perceived discrepancy between demand of the situation and capacity, and the higher the appraised cost of making such a reaction, the more stress there will be acting on the individual. The work of Selye (1966) first set the model for response theories of stress. Tache and Selye (1978) stated that "stress is the non–specific response of the body to any demand made upon it". He described stress quite equivocably as the person's response to the demands of his environment. Selye's primary concern was for the physiological mechanism and this has led to a close association between response-based and physiological models of stress. Selye's elucidation of the body's response to stress has led to a better grasp of the biochemical, anatomic, and neuro-hormonal changes that accompany adaptation to stress. In fact, three basic themes build Selye's concept of stress. First, the physiological stress response does not depend upon the nature of the stressor, and not on the organism in which it is evoked. The response syndrome represent a universal pattern of reactions which protect the person and preserves its integrity. Second, he believes that defence reactions progress in three stages, if the exposure to stress is continuous, namely alarm reactions; resistance-bodily changes marking the person's adaptation to the external force and exhaustion. The third theme of the Selye's concept of stress is that if these defence responses are severe and prolonged, it would result in disease states. However, Selye did not explicitly include cognitive or emotional factors and their impact on the adaptive processes. But it has also been observed that some noxious physical conditions do not produce the general adaptation syndrome. It has now been suggested that much of the physiological response is not directly determined by the actual presence of the stressor agent but by its psychological impact on the person.

Transactional Perspective of Stress

The transactional model of stress appears to be emerging as a broad integrative framework in this complex area. In this perspective, stress has been described as part of a complex and dynamic system of transaction between the person and his environment. It emphasizes that stress is an individual perceptual phenomenon rooted in psychological process. This model has been developed largely by Lazarus and his colleagues (Lazarus & Lunier, 1978; Lazarus & Folkman, 1984). According to this view, stress is said to occur in the face of "demands that tax or exceed the resources of the system or, to put it in slightly different way, demands to which there are no readily available adaptive responses." The transactional perspective emphasizes 'cognitive appraisals' and 'coping responses.' A stressful transaction begins with a primary cognitive appraisal that a situation requires an effective response to avoid or reduce physical or psychological threat or harm, and a secondary appraisal that no completely effective response is immediately available. The events or situations is not stressful in itself. It becomes a source of stress only when the focal person appraises it as to be a threat for him and to exceed his capability to deal with it. The person makes the best response possible and actively defines and shapes stressful transactions by means of his cognitive appraisals and coping responses. According to this model situations cannot be simply labelled as 'stressful' or 'not stressful'. They may be potentially stressful or may be stressful for such-and-such proportion of the population. To determine the existence of stress one must consider the status of the focal person in relation to his environment. This is the reason that the same situation or event is differently responded to by different persons, and even differently by the same person at different times.

The concept of stress is bound to the person, and is a subjective experience. The physical and psycho-social situations become stressors via cognitive appraisal and interpretation of the threat situations by the focal person. Lazarus' model begins when the person evaluates a particular event or situation or demand. After perceiving the situation, the focal person makes two types of appraisal at his cognitive level, i.e., primary and secondary appraisals. In primary appraisal, the individual evaluates the threats or loss likely to happen. Further, in secondary appraisal, the individual appraises his capability and resources to deal with the confronting situation. The severity of the felt stress is determined by the degree of imbalance between cognitively appraised demand or threat (CAD) and cognitively appraised supplies of the human and physical resources

(CAS). It may be formulated as: Stress = CAD > CAS. A stress reaction in the individual is the joint effect of his psychic and somatic dispositions and the stress provoking quality of situational condition. The definition extended by Appley & Trumbell (1967) fits in this model. According to them, "stressfulness of stimulus exposure or event is dependent upon the pattern of stimulus-organism interaction in a particular time and a particular place." According to Lazarus (1975), the 'general adaptation syndrome' may be precipitated not only by noxious stimuli but by the psychological reactions to physical stimuli also. McGrath (1976) has also defined stress as "an environmental situation perceived as presenting a demand which threatens to exceed person's capacities and resources for meeting it, under conditions where he expects a substantial differential in the rewards and the costs for meeting the demands versus not meeting it." The definition of stress proposed by Cox (1978) also fits in this perspective. According to him, "stress can only be sensibly defined as a perceptual phenomenon arising from a comparison between the demand on the person and his ability to cope. An imbalance in this mechanism, when coping is important, gives rise to the experience of stress, and to stress response."

Recently proposed "cognitive-affective" model of stress (Wofford & Daly, 1997) also emphasized the role of cognitive and perceptual processes in response to stress situations. The model offers a plausible explanation for why each individual's perception and response to stressful situation is a unique one. The core of their theoretical model is a cognitive-affective stress propensity (CASP) construct which consider eight individual difference variables; viz., cognitive-affective connectivity, psychological magnification, attributional style, locus of control, negative affectivity, self-esteem, private self-consciousness, and anger-irritability, as determinants of stress-strain relationships.

In fact, psychological stress in not a simple event, but is a process which comprises following successive events:

1. Perception of some unusual, demanding, noxious or adverse situation or event.

2. Cognitive appraisal by the focal person of the demands or threats, and probable undesirable consequence of the situation, and of his capabilities and available resources.

3. Emergence of a state of emotional disequilibrium spontaneously followed by deviant or unhealthy psychological, physiological and bio-chemical responses.
4. Operation of adaptive or coping efforts by the focal personal at cognitive and behavioural levels.

Stress therefore, may be referred to as a "deviant psycho-physiological state of the individual resulted from a situation cognitively appraised as excessively demanding or threatening, and requiring the focal person to make some adaptive efforts to cope with it."

Confusion about Terminology

The main confusion over the definition of stress has arisen because of disciplinary or conceptual bias of the invisible colleges. In physics, stress has a meaning or force which, acting on a body, produces strain or deformation. In physiology, the various changes in the physiological functions in response to evocative agents denote stress (rather than strain). In psychology, stress refers to a state of the organism resulted from some interaction with the environment. In psychophysiology, stress is that stimulus which imposes detectable strain that cannot be easily accommodated by the body and so presents an impairing effect on health or/and behaviour. Thus, psychophysiologists hold that stress can only be considered in terms of both stimulus and response, and influence of mild stress on health may become evident either as physical signs or mental symptoms, or both.

The stress researchers in various disciplines have used such terms as systematic stress, biological stress, psychological stress, physiological, psychological and sociological levels of stress, and social psychological stress to refer to the concept of stress. These concepts are closely related and since the limiting adjective are not always used by the scholars, they are often inter-mixed. The limiting adjectives, if used, may help in identifying:

1. The context in which the term is used : For instance, stress when used in primarily psychological contexts, is not necessarily equivalent to systematic stress.

2. The discipline of researcher and the nature of stimuli considered as stressors: For instance, physical and humoral stimuli are primarily studied in physiology and psychobiology (systematic stress) and psychological stimuli in psychology.

3. The response relevant to scientists: For instance, physiologists, primarily concerns with physiological changes; psychophysiologists with health and behaviour (produced by changes in physiological functions); and psychologists with deviations at the psychological and behavioural levels.

Thus, we see that the limiting adjectives help in delineating the various closely related stress concepts. This has been noted by several stress-researchers, and is also evident from McGrath's (1976) "social-psychological" concepts. This concept "means roughly what Cofer and Apply (1964) means by psychological as distinct from systematic stress, and what Lazarus (1966) means by psychological and sociological, as distinct from physiological, levels of stress."

In a laudable effort, Ram Chandra Rao (1983a) has highlighted the origin of stress in ancient Indian thought. Tracing it back to the 'Samakhya' and 'Yoga' systems, he pointed out two Sanskrit words 'Klesa' and 'Dukha' which correspond not only to the concept of stress in common use but also, to an extent, to the concept in its technical sense. The concept of 'Klesa' has its origin in the root 'Khis' which means 'to torment' to cause pain or 'to afflict'. The 'Klesa' is not a mental process but is a set of 'hindering load' on mental process. Thus the concept 'Klesa,' system views 'Dukha' to signify the stress that the individual experiences in the course of his interaction with the world around him. On the basis of a review of ancient Indian literature, Rao concluded that the conceptual model of appraisal of the self (Asmita), the object (Raga), and the threat (Dwesha). In fact, the cognitive appraisal constitutes the functional framework for the conceptual model of stress not only in 'Samkhya-Yoga' system but also in 'Vedanta' and 'Buddhism'. He has referred to three type of stress which 'Samkhya' speaks of viz. 'Adhyatmik' (Personal), 'Adhibhoutik' (Situational) and 'Adhidavic' (Environmental).

Occupational Stress

Stress at work resulting from increasing complexities of work and its divergent demand, has become a prominent and pervading feature of the modern organizations. The researchers in the area of organizational psychology and management have used the term job stress to denote employees' mental state aroused by a job situation or a combination of job situations perceived as presenting excessive and divergent demands. Some stress researchers have emphasized the role of job situations in their definition of job occupational stress. Caplan Cobb, and French (1975) have accordingly defined occupational stress as "any characteristics of job environment which poses a threat to the individual". Copper and Marshall (1976) have expressed that "by occupational stress is meant negative environmental factors or stressors associated with a particular job".

But some other stress researchers have tried to define it in terms of interaction between worker and work environment. The stressfulness of a job situation or a factor is determined not only by the divergent or threatening demands of the situation but by how the individual perceives and evaluates it with reference to his own capability and characteristics. The definition proposed by Margolis, Kores, and Quinn (1974) falls in this category. They defined stress as "a condition at work interacting with worker's-characteristics to disrupt his psychological or physiological homeostasis." Similarly, Beehr and Newman (1978) described job stress as "a condition wherein job related factors interact with the worker to change (disrupt or enhance) his psychological conditions such that the person is forced to deviate from normal functioning." Parasuraman and Alluto (1981) also reported that job demands, constraints, and job related events or situations were not in themselves stressful, but that they may be capable of producing psychological stress and strain, depending upon personal attributes and other factors. Allen, Hitt, and Green (1982) have defined "occupational stress as disruption in individual's psychological or/ and physiological homeostasis that force them to deviate from normal functioning in interaction with their jobs and work environment." Consistent with recent conceptualization, stress denotes the psychological state experienced by an employee when faced with demands, constraints, and/or opportunities that have important but uncertain outcomes (Beehr & Bhagat, 1985; Schuler, 1980).

Person-Environment Fit Perspective of Occupational Stress

P-E fit perspective of stress proposed by French, Rodgers and Cobb (1974) well explains the concept of stress. According to this theory poor fit or misfit between employee and his work and its environment results in stress and psychological and health strains. The theory is based on the assumption that people vary in their needs, expectations and abilities just as jobs vary in their requirements, demands and incentives. When there is poor fit between the characteristics of the employee and of the job, P-E fit theory predicts the employee's well-being will be affected. In this theory the fit is not unilateral. It is rather bilateral fit between employee and his job. Both should satisfy each other's demands or expectations. Poor or insufficient supply from either side would cause stress. One form of fit involves the discrepancy between the needs and aspirations of the employee and the supplies in the job and environment to meet his needs and goals. A good P-E fit occurs when the supplies in the environment (i.e., money, support from superiors and colleagues, opportunities to satisfy needs for affiliation, power and achievement) are sufficient to satisfy the motives of the employee.

Second form of fit involves the relationship between the requirements and demands of the job and the abilities of the employee to meet those demands. If the demands of the job exceed the abilities of the employees or does not match with the temperament and interests of the employees, it will cause stress and results in psychological strain. If supplies for the motives of the person are threatened by discrepancies between demands and abilities, the individuals will experience stress. P-E fit theory emphasises the causal relationship between misfit and strains. Though the exact contents and process of the relationship of the two is not very clear, it is assumed that severity of the strains caused from misfit is determined by following factors: (i) needs which are not being satisfied, (ii) abilities to meet the job demands, (iii) the genetic and socio-cultural background of the employee, (iv) defence and coping predispositions, and (v) situational constraints on particular responses.

In fact, the degree of P-E fit can be determined objectively or subjectively. Objective P-E fit refers to fit between the objective person and the objective environment, i.e., fit independent of individual's perception of it. Subjective P-E fit refers to the fit between subjective person and the subjective environment, i.e., the individual's perception of P-E fit. P-E fit represents the interaction of the person and the environment rather than an outcome which each cause. The central theme of the theory was that misfit of either kind results in stress and threat to well-being of the focal employee. Harrison (1976) also accepted and proved validity of the P-E fit model of job stress. Ross and Altmair (1994) have also defined occupational stress in the P-E fit framework. According to them, "occupational stress is the result of interaction of work conditions with characteristics of the worker such that demands of the work exceeds the ability of the worker to cope with them." McGrath has described occupational stress as an environmental situation perceived as presenting a job demand which seems to exceed the capacity and resources of the employee to meet or deal with it. However, the nature and severity of occupational stress may be more adequately and conveniently understood observing physical and psychological symptoms which occur in the employee under the condition of job stress. Beehr and Newman (1976) have outlined three categories of these symptoms.

Psychological Symptoms: Those emotional and cognitive problems that occur under conditions of job stress

Psychological symptoms of occupational stress include job dissatisfaction, disliking for the job, depression, anxiety, boredom, frustration, isolation and resentment. Having these problems, the employee is less, able to cope with job problems in ways that would improve his work conditions and enhance his mental outlook.

***Physical Symptoms*:** Though it is difficult to know how much these physical symptoms have been caused by a particular job stress versus other aspects of employee's life, it has been established that consistent job stress links with certain physical symptoms and diseases. Among the common physical symptoms of occupational stress are cardiovascular diseases, gastrointestinal problems, allergies and skin diseases, headaches and respiratory diseases.

***Behavioural Symptoms*:** The behavioural symptoms of job stress can be classified in two categories. The first category of the symptoms belongs to the focal employees, while the other belongs to the organization. The employee-centered symptoms are avoidance of work, increased intake of alcohol or drugs, overeating or undereating, aggression towards coworkers or family members, and interpersonal problems in general. The organization related symptoms of job stress include absenteeism, leaving the job, accident proneness, and decrease in work efficiency.

Empirical research on social psychological factors in stress has been somewhat inconclusive. Nevertheless, McGrath (1976) has adduced following six general themes or propositions about job stress from the available research literature:

1. Subjectively experienced stress is contingent upon the person's perception of the situation. The subjectively experienced stress are greatly influenced by the person's interpretation of the "objective" or external stress situation.

2. Past experience can operate to affect the level of subjectively experienced stress from a given situation, or to modify reactions to that stress.

3. Positive and negative reinforcements can operate

to reduce or enhance the level of subjectively experienced stress from a given situation.

4. There is a non-linear, perhaps inverted U-shaped, relationship between degree of stress and level or quality of performance.

5. The nature of task in which person is involved, and the relationship of those task activities to the stress condition, influence the direction and shape of relationship between experienced stress and performance.

6. The presence or absence of, and the activities of, other persons in the situation influence both the subjectively experienced stress and behaviour in response to stress.

Organizational Role Stress

Recent years have seen an increased interest in the use of role theory, to describe and explain the stresses associated with membership in organization. The concept of "role" is the key concept in understanding the integration of the individual in a system. The first requirement in linking individual and organization is to locate the individual in the total set of ongoing relationship and behaviours comprised by the organization. Every organization is composed of a number of positions and specific roles associated with these positions. Katz and Kahn (1966) have accordingly extended that an organization is a system of roles. Position or office is essentially a relational concept, defining one position in terms of its relationship to other and to the system as a whole. Each position in the organization is associated with a set of avtivities, which constitute the role being performed by the person occupying that position. In fact, no role is totally independent and sufficient in itself. Performance of one's role is determined also by the patterns of interpersonal connectedness within which that role-behaviour takes place. This implies that roles are not tied to any specific milieu or setting, but to other transcend settings. A role is normally enacted in relation to many other offices/positions in the organization.

It may be directly related to certain others, less directly to still others, and only remotely concerned to remaining offices in the organization. These offices make up the 'role set' for that particular role. The persons occupying various positions in the role set have a' stake in role performance of the focal person. They develop beliefs and attitudes about what the focal person should and should not do as part of his role. These prescriptions and proscriptions held by the members of a role set are designated as 'role expectation'. Role performance of a person is evaluated by the members of role set in expectations as communicated, directly or indirectly, to the focal person. These communicated expectations are referred to as 'sent role'. Thus we may define job role as "a set of specific normative activities, associated with a position, to be performed in the framework of expectations, prescriptions and proscriptions, held by the members of the role set".

Normally, performance of a role satisfies various needs of its occupant. But sometimes it becomes a potential source of stress too for the role-occupant. The problem a role-occupant faces today is that of managing the complex structure of roles by achieving an integration of one's self with the system of other roles as well as integration of various roles a person may be occupying. Interest in organizational role stress has increased a great deal in recent years. Kahn, Wolfe, Quinn, Sonek, and Rosenthal (1964) were the earliest to draw attention to organizational stress in general and role stress in particular. These researchers, after systematic exploration, identified two basic sources of role stress, i.e., role conflict and role ambiguity.

Role Conflict

Role conflict arises when various members of the role set, hold quite different or conflicting role expectations toward a focal person. They may impose pressures on that focal person toward different kinds of behaviour at a time. To the extent that these different role pressures (expectations) give rise to role forces within him, he will experience a psychological conflict. Actual degree of objective role conflict depends on the configuration of role pressures actually exerted by role senders (member of the role set) on the role-occupant. Kahn et al (1964) have described six types of role conflicts, namely, sent role conflict, intra-sender conflict, inter-sender conflict, inter-role conflict,. person-role conflict, and role overload.

Sent role Conflict: It is defined as the simultaneous occurrence of two or more sets of pressures such that compliance with one would make it more difficult to comply with the other. In its extreme form, compliance with one set of pressures makes the compliance with another set completely impossible; the two sets of pressures are mutually contradictory. Here in fact, role conflicts has been taken as environmental (objective) variable. The intensity or magnitude of a person's role conflict depends on the absolute and relative strength of the opposing forces. But the actual magnitude of psychological conflict a focal personnel experiences, is determined by his personal attributes.

Intra-sender Conflict: It arises when opposing expectations are held by a single member of the role set, for example, a supervisor instructs his subordinates to work faster and also to improve the quality of product.

Inter-sender Conflict: It denotes the role conflict resulting from opposing role expectations from two or more members of role set. Pressures from one role sender are in conflict with the pressures exerted by other role senders. For example, management wants the workers to stick to their duty while the labour union calls for a strike.

Inter-role Conflict: It occurs when role pressures associated with membership in an organization or institution are in conflict with expectations stemming from membership in other groups or institutions. For example, the family responsibilities of a person conflict with his job responsibilities.

Person-role Conflict: It exists when there is conflict between needs and values of an employee and the demands of his job role. It can occur when role requirements violate moral values of an employee. In another case of person-role conflict, the person's needs and aspiration may lead to behaviours which are unacceptable to the members of his role set.

Role Overload: It is a very prevalent form of role conflict in industrial organizations. Overload could be regarded as a kind of inter-sender conflict in which various role senders may hold quite legitimate expectations that a person performs a wide variety of tasks, all of which are mutually compatible in the abstract. But it may be virtually impossible for the focal person to complete all of them within given time limits. He is likely to experience overload as a conflict of priorities. He must decide which pressure to comply with and which to hold off. If it is impossible to deny any of the pressures, he may be taxed beyond the limits of his abilities. This overload involves a kind of person-role conflict, and is perhaps best regarded as a complex, emergent type, combining aspects of inter-sender and person-role conflicts.

Role Ambiguity

Much of role conflict can be thought of as a kind of inadequate role sending: lack of agreement or coordination among role senders. Another pattern of inadequacy in role sending, causing stress, constitutes role ambiguity. Each member of an organization must have certain kinds of information at his disposal in order to perform his job adequately and smoothly. He must also know the potential consequences of his role performance and non-performance for himself, his role sender, and for the organization in general. Non-availability of the adequate informations about the above mentioned job-aspect, causes role stress to the focal employee. Actually, role ambiguity is a direct function of the discrepancy between the information available to the employee and that which is required for adequate performance of his job role. It may be noted that each of the above-mentioned forms of role ambiguity may exhibit a reciprocal causal relationship with dimensions of role conflict. Thus, even though role conflict and role ambiguity are conceptually distinguishable types of role stress, one should not necessarily expect their empirical indices to be unrelated.

Besides the objective or organizational causes of role ambiguity, there may be subjective counterparts of ambiguity. The subjective or experienced ambiguity is a state of the focal person. It is the expected consequence of objective ambiguity, but the relationship is less than perfect. There may be individual differences in perception of and responses to ambiguities. Employees with tendency of intolerance for ambiguity (Frenkel-Brunswik, 1949) and need for cognition—a need for clear, orderly, and meaningful cognitive experience (Cohen, Scotland and Wolfe, 1955) are likely to experience more ambiguity and therefore more anxiety and strain.

The extent to which required information are communicated clearly and consistently to a focal person, will tend to induce in him an experience of certainty with respect to his role requirements and his position in the organization. To the extent such informations are lacking the will experience ambiguity. The relationship between the objective ambiguity and the intensity of the ambiguity experienced by the person are modified by his various personal attributes.

Kahn and Quinn (1970) suggested that role ambiguity may be regarding activities, responsibilities, personal style and norms. They have also suggested that four different kinds of roles are likely to experience ambiguity: roles new to the organization, roles in expanding or contracting organizations, roles in organizations exposed to frequent changes in demand, and roles on process. On the basis of its causes are role stress classified under three main headings: (i) expectation generated stress, are which includes role conflict and role ambiguity, (ii) expectation resources discrepancies, which includes role overload, responsibility, authority dilemma, and inadequate technical information, (iii) stresses resulted from interaction between role and personal characteristics of the focal person.

Another important potential stressor associated with one's organizational role, besides role conflict and ambiguity, is 'responsibility for people' (Cooper & Marshall, 1976). Increased responsibility for people frequently meant that one has to spend more time on interacting with others, maintaining coordination, attending meetings, and in consequence more time in trying to meet deadline pressures and schedules. It has been noted that physical stress was linked to the level of responsibility. It has also been observed that responsibility for people was related to heavy smoking, diastolic blood pressure, serum cholesterol level and symptoms of coronary heart disease. Lack of participation in decision making, lack of managerial support, having to keep pace with increasing standards of performance and coping with rapid technological change have also been mentioned as potential role stressors by Cooper and Marshall.

Framework of Occupational Stress

The nature of occupational stress can be more conveniently and clearly understood in the framework of its causes, mediators, moderators and consequences. It is generally assumed that unchecked stress of job life reduce performance, job satisfaction and morale and cause absenteeism and turnover. But, in fact, job stress does not directly affect the job behaviour of the focal worker. The experience and consequences of stress are mediated and moderated by several psychological and situational factors. Ivancevich and Matteson (1987) have proposed a framework of occupational stress which is rigorous enough to analyze and understand job stress and its effects, and to evolve meaningful and practical strategies to manage job stress in Figure 1.1. The framework emphasizes stress in a dynamic system of transaction between the person and his work and non-work environment. The framework illustrates that a feedback loop links stressors and outcomes which illustrates a cyclical rather than a linear stress system.

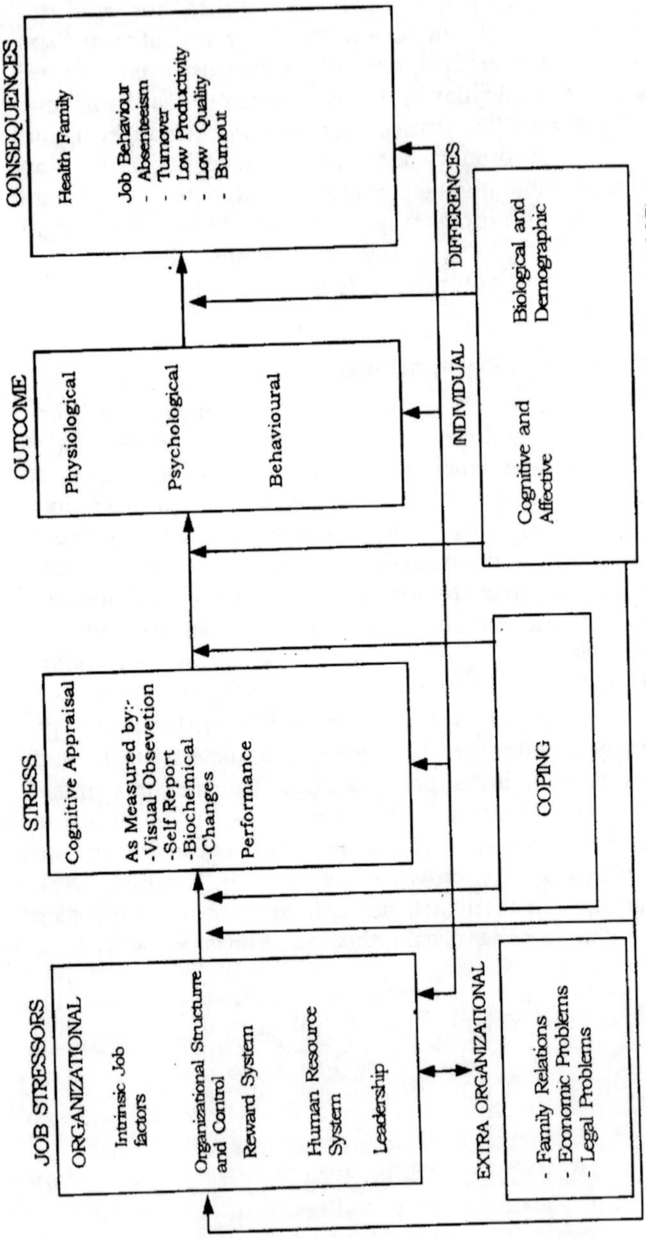

Fig. 1.1. Occupational Stress Framework (Ivancevich and Matteson, 1987).

Approaches To The Study of Job Stress

There has been a lot of controversy regarding the actual meaning of the concept of stress. The basic reason behind this controversy was that stress researchers in different disciplines have different referents for the term stress. Even if everyone used the term in same meaning, there would still be differences in approaches to the study of stress. There are at present at least four approaches to studying and treating occupational stress. These four approaches typically focus the stressors of job life and consequent strains. These approaches also recommend different target and types of treatment for alleviating the problems resulted from job stress. The following Table 1.1 outlines the four identified approaches to the study of occupational stress (Beehr & Frang, 1987).

TABLE 1.1
Approaches to the Study of Occupational Stress

Approach	*Typical*	*Typical Outcome*	*Typical Primary Target of Treat ment*
Medical	Physical	Physical Strain	Individual
Clinical Counselling Psychology	Psycho-logical	Psychological Strain	Individual
Engineering Psychology	Physical	Job Performance	Organization
Organizat-ional Psychology	Psycho-logical	Psychological Strain	Organization

The medical approach, having its roots in the tradition of Cannon and Selye, focus on physical causes and consequences of job stress. The typical primary target of treatment for this approach is individual. Here the treatment of the focal person is done through application of medication. This approach did not develop from primary interest in occupational or workplace, though it is applied to them.

The psychological approach to occupational stress

emphasizes psychological causes and consequence of stress. The approach is labelled as clinical or counselling psychology approach and involves the treatment of depression or anxiety through counselling or psychotherapy. This approach also like medical approach, was not developed specifically for dealing with the stress prevailing in the workplace.

The third approach, i.e., clinical or counselling psychology, adopted to the study of occupational stress focus on physical characteristics of the work and workplace as stressors and as job performance as the typical outcome (strain). This approach has implications for the physical design of the work and workplace as treatments. In this approach the typical primary target of treatment remains the organization, not the individual.

The organizational psychology approach accepts that psychological variable prevailing in the organizations cause psychological strains. In this approach typical target of treatment is making necessary changes or modifications in the organization or the characteristics of workplace. This approach was developed with specific interest in workplace stress.

However, people working in the field of occupational stress from either of these four perspectives try to broaden their approaches to take the important characteristics of job stress from other approaches into consideration, but they focus on the area in which they have the most expertise. Since these approaches to the study of job stress have developed largely independently from each other, it should not be expected that they use terms in the same manner.

2
SOURCES OF OCCUPATIONAL STRESS

Though occupational stress initially arises from constituent factors of job and its psycho-physical environment, these factors are not inherently stressors. In fact, personal characteristics of the employee and his cognitive appraisal of the job factors in the framework of his capacity and resources determine the extent of stress he would experience from a job factor or situation. This is the reason that we can only hypothetically predict the potency of the job factors or situations for causing stress, but we cannot categorize or generalize any work-setting variable as a universal stressor. However, some job factors or work conditions such as extreme heat or cold, chronic dangers, demotion, loss of job, etc., are likely to cause stress to majority of the workers. But stress resulted from these factors also vary from one worker to another. The pressures caused from the job factors, in fact, are mediated by the personal characteristics of the focal worker. Moreover, certain psychological and behavioural specialities of the employee also become consistent sources of stress to him. Thus, we can broadly classify all the sources of occupational stress in two categories, i.e., individual characteristics and work setting variables.

Individual Characteristics

Personality characteristics of the employees are one of the most prominent factors which interfere with their job behaviour. Employees' responses to work demands and pressures are largely influenced by their personality characteristics, and psychological and behavioural patterns, such as believes and values, aspiration and expectancy, need structure, attributions, locus of control, personality traits, coping skills, cognitive patterns, etc. An important personal characteristic which influence the experience of stress is "sense of control". Control refers to the perception by the individual worker that his or her action results in expected outcomes, particularly those which are important for the workers. Sense of control has been found to have significant effect on people's response to stress. Sense of control (ability to self-pace in work) over task and work environment cause fewer symptoms of stress (Frankenheuser & Johanson, 1986). Individuals with hardy personality are likely to experience less stress and strains because of this characteristics of commitment, and capability of control and facing challenges (Kobasa, 1979). Low level of tolerance and patience, rigidity, low self-esteem, high anxiety, intra-psychic conflicts, external locus of control, and certain cognitive patterns enhance employee's susceptibility, to experience more stress as well as strain.

Personality traits of employees play a significant role in determining the severity of job stress experienced by them. Though personality characteristics and traits are generally not the source of stress, they mediate the stress and moderate the strains. In a recent study Srivastava and Veena (1999), on a sample of industrial supervisors, noted that supervisors rating higher on emotionality, dependence and sensitivity, and imaginativeness, experienced comparatively higher degree of occupational stress. Employees' cognitive appraisal of job stressors were also found to be influenced by their personality attributes.

High anxiety also is a frequent source as well as promoter of stress. Anxiety has also been reported as an immediate outcome of felt stress. In the last three decades, anxiety and stress have become the topics of intense interest among psychologists and laymen. Anxiety has been variously defined as stimulus, response, drive, motive, and trait. Anxiety is a vague fear associated with the emotions of terror, horror, alarm, fright, panic and dread.

It has also been characterized by the feelings of uncertainty and helplessness in an adverse situation. These feelings and emotions associated with anxiety cause stress, and also enhance the severity of stress by influencing their cognitive appraisals. Indicating the relationship of anxiety to stress, Speilberger (1979) has stated that in a transaction between person and environment, stressors are linked to anxiety reactions by perception of threat. In interactional model of anxiety (Endler, 1975, 1980), stress has been defined as a situational variable, the perception of which is influenced by the individual's predisposition to react to stress with increased anxiety. The perception of stress in turn increases the level of anxiety of the focal person. Trait-anxiety plays prominent role in the experience of stress and reactions to it. Trait anxiety is an abiding predisposition and is a relatively stable characteristic which influence individual's behaviour to a great extent. Trait anxiety refers to people's disposition or tendency to perceive a wide range of situations as threatening and to respond to these situations with differential elevations in state anxiety (Speilberger, 1975). Thus, we see that anxiety is a source of stress as well as elevator of the stress and a resultant of felt stress.

Employees' locus of control has also been noted to determine the degree of occupational stress experienced by them. In a number of studies, external locus of control has been reported to be associated with higher degree of stress and anxiety. In a study on a sample of banking personnel, Srivastava and Krishna (1992) noted that employees with external locus of control experience comparatively higher degree of occupational stress, and lower job satisfaction. Employees with external locus of control have also been found to be more alienated from work setting and less involved in their job.

Employees' job attributions also determine the extent of stress they experience in their job life. In a recent study Gupta (1999) noted that employees attributing to their efforts, nature of job activities, work conditions, and managerial policy for their success and failures in job life experienced higher role stress as compared to those who attributed to chance or luck for their achievements and failures at work.

Besides mediating the effect of stressors, certain behavioural patterns become direct source of stress. "Type A Behavioural Patterns" (Friedman & Rosenman, 1974) are the examples of such behavioural sources of occupational stress. Type A Behavioural Patterns, such as drive to achieve more and more, aggressive striving, high competitiveness, high hostility, hyper alertness, rapid pace in themselves cause stress and become risk factors in certain somatic problems, particularly coronary heart disease. Type A people may be resentful and suspicious of others and may easily be angered by people in their environment. In order to achieve more and more, these people ignore the feelings of others.

Employees' age, sex, health, status, experience, and socio-cultural background have also been found to influence the experience of occupational stress. Variety of social supports (such as emotional, tangible, informational and esteem supports) have also been reported by stress researchers as dominant mediators of the experiences of occupational stress, as well as moderator (buffer) of the relationship between occupational stress and consequent strains. Cognitive coping has also been reported as mediating the experience of strains. Intellectualization, rationalization, and reversal of effect, moderate the severity of stress, while cognitive avoidance and denial might bring temporary relief from the stress but cause severe strain in long term.

Work Setting Variables

Job Role : Job role is a major source of satisfaction as well as frustration for the employees. Certain characteristics or inadequacies of job role have been noted as prominent source of occupational stress. Researchers have applied "role theory" to understanding stress problems at work and to examining how role pressures contribute to occupational stress. Ivancevich and Matteson (1980) noted that role pressure occurs when an employees' expectations or demands conflict with expectation and demands of the organization. Kahn and his associates

(1964) have extensively investigated and discussed the stresses arising from two major characteristics of organizational roles, i.e., role ambiguity and role conflict, (inter-sender, intra-sender, inter-role and person-role conflicts). Role overload and role under-load have also been noted as occupational stressors. The features of job role and role set which cause occupational stress have been discussed in details in previous chapter.

Pareek (1981) on the basis of theoretical speculation and statistical analysis has identified following ten situations of role stress:

1. Inter-Role Distance: Individual occupies more than one role at a time. His occupational role may come into conflict with family or social roles. These conflicts among different roles represent inter-role distance.

2. Role Stagnation: This kind of stress is the result of gap between demand outgrow of previous role to occupy new roles effectively. With advance of an individual his role also grows and changes. With this change in role, the need for taking his new role becomes crucial. This is the problem of role growth. This becomes an acute problem specially when an individual enters new roles after occupying a role for a long period.

3. Role Expectation Conflict: This type of stress arises when two or more members of one's role set impose opposing expectations on the role occupant and he is ambivalent as to whom to please. Stress is created also if the same member holds opposing expectations toward the focal person.

4. Role Erosion: This type of role stress is the function of the role occupant's feeling that some functions which should properly be the part of his role are transferred to or being performed by some other. This can also happen when the functions are performed by the role occupant but the credit goes to someone else.

5. Role Overload: When the role occupant feels that there are too many expectations from the significant members in his role set, he experiences role overload.

There are two aspects of this stress: quantitative and qualitative. The former refers to having 'too much to do' while latter refers to 'too difficult to do'.

6. Role Isolation: This situation of role stress arises from psychological distance between the occupant's role and other roles in the same role set. The main criteria of role isolation is frequency of interaction with other roles in the role set. In the absence of strong linkage, the stress of role isolation may be high. The gap between the desired and the existing linkage would indicate the degree of role isolation.

7. Personal Inadequacy: Role stress also arises when the role occupant feels that he does not have the necessary skills and training for effectively performing the function expected from his role. This is found to happen when proper placements are not made and the organization do not impart periodic training to enable the employees to cope with the fast changes both within and outside the organization.

8. Self-Role Distance: When the expectations from one's role goes against his self-concept, he feels this kind of stress. This is essentially a conflict arising out of incongruence between personal attributes of an employee and the requirement of his job role.

9. Role Ambiguity: Role ambiguity arises when the individual is not clear about various expectations people have from his role. Role ambiguity may also be due to lack of information regarding role and its enactment to the role occupant.

10. Resource Inadequacy: This type of role stress is evident when the role occupant feels that he is not provided with adequate resources for smoothly performing the functions expected from his role.

Job Characteristics and Attributes

Characteristics of the job the are a very common source of employees' satisfactions, frustrations, and stress. Task complexity and difficulty, quantitative and qualitative demands of the job, and employees' controllability over task are the frequent sources of occupational stress. The pace at which an employee is required to do work is one of the characteristics of the job causing stress to the employee. Work pace is concerned with who or what controls the speed of work. Another way to say it is the extent of control an employee has over the work process. This pacing may be controlled either by machine or human being. The employee might also control the pacing himself. If there is machine pacing the employee has to become a machine, which causes stress to the employee. Another source of stress integral to this system is the lack of control over the work process. The pressure of repetitive work in machine pacing system gradually becomes a continuous source of stress to the worker.

Another important characteristic of the job is its attributes, which refer to the extent of opportunity it provides to satisfy various needs of the employees, such as autonomy, social interaction, power and autonomy, use of knowledge and abilities, etc. If the jobs lack enrichment and provide little opportunity to satisfy these needs, they become stressful to their incumbents.

Physical Work Condition and Technology

Another set of factors in work setting which cause stress are related to qualities of physical work environment and technology. Inadequate, taxing, or hazardous physical conditions at work, such as insufficient or excessive lighting, continued loud noise, extreme cold or heat, fluctuation in temperature, crowded workplace, etc. These physical qualities of work environment cause direct sensory stress and indirect psychological stress through their potentiality for causing negative health consequences. Technical limitations, rapid change in technology, inadequate technical management, incongruence among task, technology and organisational structure, inadequate man-machine system, and mechanization of man are the potential sources of stress prevailing in work setting.

Performance Feedback and Reward System

Performance feedback is another important factor which enhances employees' motivation and performance, but causes dissatisfaction and stress if it is inadequate or absent. If the feedback is not given at adequate time or it is less frequent, it is likely to cause stress to the concerned worker. Reward or incentives which workers receive for their work also play an important role in enhancing employees' motivation and performance. But if it is not adequate, it is likely to cause frustration and stress to the worker. The rewards for better or exceptional job performance include monetary compensation or benefits, recognition, appreciation, privilege and promotion. These non-financial rewards are usually more effective in improving employees' motivation and performance level. If the workers feel they are not being adequately, proportionately or timely rewarded for their performance, they are likely to encounter stress. These rewards become less effective or ineffective if they are not given at the proper time.

Interpersonal Relations at Work

The quality of interpersonal relationship at work plays a dominant role in determining employees' job behaviour and job strains. It has been consistently linked to job stress (Payne, 1980). Kets de Vries (1984) reported that at least three types of interpersonal relationships have been studied, viz., relationship with co-workers, relationship within work groups, and relationship with supervisors or superiors. As the social support form the co-workers and work groups, and supervisors buffers the job stress and consequent strains, the poor or strained interpersonal relationships at work is associated with the feeling of threat for the employees. Poor co-worker relationships are associated with low trust, supportiveness and interest or willingness to listen (French & Caplan, 1973). When employees have poor relationship with co-workers, they blame the job stress they experience on their co-workers. Conversely, those workers who report a greater amount of group cohesion are more able to cope with stress on the job (Kets de Vries, 1984). Relationship with supervisor or leaders are equally important in determining the amount of job stress. Certain aspects of this relationship have been identified as potentially affecting job stress. First, having considerate leadership style allows the employees to participate in decision making, and good two-way communications. Researches have revealed that considerate leadership helps employees in dealing with job stress. Poor relationship between workers and supervisor does not cause stress only to the workers but also to the supervisor to a considerable extent.

Another potentially stressful relationship within the workplace is observed in interactions with customers or clients. These relationships often present a primary focus on the work an employee does. One group of employees who have been identified as being at risk for experiencing job stress are those who are involved in providing service to others (Schuler, 1984). For example, the medical personnel having more contact with patients, report high level of emotional exhaustion (Maslach & Jackson, 1981).

Organization Structure and Climate

Besides the role and job characteristics, certain features of the structure, climate, and culture of the organization also cause severe psychological stress to its members. The potential effects of the structure of an organization on individual performance and job attitudes have only recently been studied and better understood. The extent to which individual employees are involved in direction and decision making in their work leads to the definition of two kinds of organizational structures: centralized (tall organization) and decentralized (flat organization). It is generally observed that the structure which allows employees more decision making power produces less stress. Ivancevich and Donnely (1975) in their study noted that employees in flat organization reported less job stress and more job satisfaction. This differential effects might be linked to the fact that decision making enhances the meaningfulness an employees finds in work and provides the employees with a greater sense of autonomy, responsibility, certainty, control and ownership (Schuler, 1980; Cooper, 1987).

Climate and culture of the organization has also been found to be the source of satisfaction and stress. Culture of the organization is defined as to refer to the beliefs and expectations shared by the members of the organizations. An important stress that results from organizational culture is the existence of competition. For instance, as organizations decline, specially in relation to downsizing and budget cut, five job stressors emerge, namely, feeling of job insecurity, work overload because of unrealistic deadlines, underutilization of employees skills, promotional obstacles, and intra-and inter-group competitions (Jick, 1985). Many workers feel stress due to power struggles or office politics prevailing in the organization. Office politics are said to be an important factor in number of organizational practices, viz., promotions and transfers, allocation of supplies or equipment, division of authority and coordination between high level managers. Managers who are engaged in power games and political alliances can place stressful expectations and demands on subordinates (Matteson & Ivancevich, 1987). Cooper and Melhuish (1980) reported "relationship within the organization", and "poor organizational climate" to be causing stress and health strains among executives. In a study Srivastava (1990) found that inadequate organizational climate was positively correlated with the symptoms of mental ill-health among its employees.

Another factor of organizational climate which might cause stress to its employees involve territory or personal space. Organizational territory is defined as the personal space or area of activities within which an employee works (Ivancevich & Matteson, 1980). Territoriality has been identified as a powerful stressor for workers (French & Caplan, 1973). Territoriality cause stress by arousing the feeling of alienation or isolation in new or distant department.

Occupational Stress in Public and Private Sector Organizations

Structure and climate of the public and private sector organizations markedly differ, and so are likely to cause different amount of stress to its members. In a study

Pestonjee and Singh (1978) noted that managers in the private enterprises rated higher on role stress. Similar results were revealed in the studies conducted by Singh (1987), Sharma and Shudershan (1983), and Singh (1989). But in a study Banerjea (1989) observed public sector employees experiencing comparatively more job stress.

In an extensive study Srivastava (1990) examined the effect of overall nature (structure, systems, climate and culture) of the organization on employees occupational stress. To test the hypothesis, employees operating in public and private sector organizations were compared with regard to their occupational stress.

The results (Table 2.1) make it apparent that employees (three levels taken together) operating in the public and private sector organizations significantly differ with regard to the stress they perceive arising from various components of their jobs. The results clearly indicated that employees belonging to the public sector organizations experienced markedly higher stress stemming from most of the components of their job, such as role ambiguity, role conflict, group pressures, responsibility for persons, supervision and control, underparticipation, powerlessness, poor peer-relations, unprofitability, low status, strenuous work conditions, and intrinsic impoverishment. But surprisingly no significant difference could be observed between the employees of the two enterprises so far as the stress of role overload was concerned. It was also noted that powerlessness, underparticipation, and low-profitability were among the predominant job stressors for the public sector employees. Whereas the private sector employees perceived responsibility for persons, low-profitability and role overload as prominent job stressors. On the other hand, intrinsic impoverishment, low status, and poor peer-relation were rated quite low as job stressors by the employees in both types of organizations.

Table 2:1
Occupational Stress of The Employees in Public And Private Sector Organizations

Occupational Stressor	*Public Sector* (N=450)		*Private Sector* (N=450)		
	Mean	S.D.	*Mean*	S.D.	*t*
Role Overload	18.68	4.81	18.45	4.27	01.09
Role Ambiguity	11.69	3.36	10.49	2.73	05.87**
Role Conflict	15.13	2.91	13.09	2.99	10.37**
Grp. Pressures	12.85	3.58	11.42	2.62	06.85**
Resp. for Persons	09.22	2.78	09.85	2.16	03.75**
Under-participation	13.85	3.20	10.85	2.64	15.32**
Powerlessness	10.66	3.03	08.76	2.16	10.89**
Poor Peer-Relations	11.83	3.10	09.78	2.30	11.25**
Intrinsic Impoverishment	11.12	3.22	09.58	2.56	07.90**
Low Status	08.62	2.76	07.58	2.08	06.38**
Stren. Work Condition	10.43	3.46	10.24	2.43	00.97
Low profitability	06.89	2.58	06.18	1.76	04.78**
Overall Occupational Stress	140.98	21. 81	126.17	17.24	11.30**

** $P < .01$

Organizational Change

Organizations in the global market place are continuously changing. These consistent changes in organisational structure and its functioning are the results of advancements in technology, economic constraints, and rational competitions. Although most of these changes are necessary and long overdue, the downside includes the risk of huge cost in terms of increased health care expenses, lost productivity, and lower level of job satisfaction. This cost may be directly attributed to the distress that is created when an organization's employees encounter consistent changes. These changes at organizational level cause stress at individual level. As a response to the struggling economy, intense foreign competitions, and need to compete on a global basis, organizations have been right-sized, re-engineered and restructured on a massive scale. The organizational change occur when the company alters the way it does business, such as computerizing the processes and entering a new market or product line. In the environment of organizational changes, the employees are being required to adopt to the changes in order to accommodate or facilitate the needs of the organization (Lawler, 1994). In a changing environment, employees are in a consistent state of slush, uncertainty and insecurity, which lead to occupational stress. These changes stress the employees by forcing them to function in a different manner and in different environment. Johnson and Sarason (1979) have argued that change, depending upon how it is perceived, is one of the primary causes of stress, and organizational change can be extremely stressful due to the feeling of insecurity it evokes. However, the relationship between organizational change and employees stress has not been extensively investigated. In a recent article, Mack, Nelson, and Quick (1998) argued that the impact of organizational change is an individual phenomenon. Individual's psychological, cognitive and perceptual process play an important role in mediating the experience of and reactions to the stress of organizational change. They have suggested to understand the stress of organizational change in the framework of "Cognitive-Affective Stress Propensity" (CAP) construct proposed by Wofford and Daly (1997). This model is in the line of individual difference tradition and explains why there is individual variance in perception of and reactions to stressful situations. Each employee evaluates the changes by filtering it through his/her own unique perceptual process and the potential impact of the change is determined by this evaluation.

Other Sources of Occupational Stress

McGrath (1976) has suggested the following six sources

of occupational stress:

(i) Task-based stress (difficulty, ambiguity, load, etc.).
(ii) Role-based stress (conflict, ambiguity, load, etc.).
(iii) Stress intrinsic to behaviour setting (e.g., effect of crowding or undermanning, etc.).
(iv) Stress arising from the physical environment itself (e.g., extreme hot/cold, hostile forces, etc.).
(v) Stress arising from social environment in sense of interpersonal relations (e.g., interpersonal disagreement, privacy, isolation, etc.).
(vi) Stress within the person system, which the fòcal person brings with him to the situation (e.g., anxiety, perceptual style, motivation, experience, etc.).

Cooper and Marshall (1976) have described following seven categories of the sources of managerial stress:

(i) Factors intrinsic to the job: Work overload underload, poor physical working conditions, time pressure, having too many decisions to make.

(ii) Career development: Overpromotion, underpromotion, lack of job security, fear of redundancy, thwarted ambition.

(iii) Role in the organization: Role ambiguity, role conflict, responsibility for people.

(iv) Relationships at work: Poor relations with boss, colleagues, and subordinates, lack of trust and supportiveness, difficulties in delegating responsibilities.

(v) Organizational structure and climate: Lack of effective consultation, restrictions on behaviour, poor communication, no sense of belonging and little or no participation in decision making.

(vi) Extra-organizational sources: Family problems, conflict of personal belief with that of company, conflict of company with family demands, marriage patterns, and relocation and mobility.

(vii) Characteristics of the individual: Type A personality, extremes of competitiveness, striving for achievement, impatience, haste, hyper-alertness, low self-esteem, lack of ability to cope or adapt to stress situation, etc.

Gross (1970) classified organizational stressors under three categories, viz., organizational careers, task, and organizational structure. Landy and Trumbo (1976) have reported job insecurity, excessive competition, hazardous working conditions, task demands, and large or unusual working hours as major sources of job stress. Factors intrinsic to job, i.e., paced-repetitive work, lack of opportunities to use valued skills and abilities, and high costs and penalties for mistakes have been indicated as stressors in the work setting (Kornhauser, 1965; Buck, 1972). Time constraint (Hall & Lawler, 1970), heavy work load (Buck, 1972), excessive and inconvenient work hours (Kornhauser, 1965; Mott et al., 1972) have also been reported as sources of job stress. Quick and Quick (1979) have emphasized the role of interpersonal factors in creating stress at work. Conflict between individuals because of incompatible goals or substantive issues on the one hand, and emotional issues on the other create stress. Small groups may also apply pressure upon their members for conformity to norms that are in conflict with member's needs, values and standards. These pressures cause occupational stress.

Parasuraman and Alluto (1981) proposed an integrated model for investigating simultaneously the relationship of contextual, task, and role-related variables to stressors, viz., inter-unit conflict, technical problems, efficiency problems, role frustrations, staff shortage, and too many meetings in the work environment. They reported that job demands, constraints, and job related events or situations were not in themselves stressful, but that they may be capable of producing psychological stress, and strain, depending on personal attributes and other coexisting factors.

Srivastava and Singh (1981) identified twelve factors which cause occupational stress, such as: role overload, role ambiguity, role conflict, group pressures, low profitability, under participation, low status, responsibility for people, intrinsic impoverishment, strenuous work condition, poor peer-relations, and powerlessness.

Besides the stressors prevailing in work setting, a number of non-work or off-the-job factors are the indirect sources of occupational stress. Models of work-non-work stress (Bhagat et al., 1985) posit that total amount of stress and strain experienced by a person is a function of both work and non-work stresses. Non-work domain is composed of a number of life domains including family, leisure/ recreational, community, social, political, religious roles.

The stresses and strains of non-work life domains influence cognitive evaluations of and reactions to the stresses of job life. Greenhaus and Parasuraman (1987) have demonstrated that non-work stresses influence and intensify the occupational stress in three ways: (*i*) additive effect of non-work stressors; (*ii*) spillover effect of non-work stresses and strains; (*iii*) interactive effect of work-non-work conflict. However, despite the inclusion of non-work factors as potential stressors in some models of work stress (Cooper & Marshall, 1976; Ivancevich & Matteson, 1980), only a few empirical studies have investigated the relationship of non-work stressors to job stress and other job related strains. Researchers have noted that life stresses were associated with decreased life satisfaction and increased job strain, job alienation, and turnover (Bhagat, et. al, 1985; Sarason & Johnson, 1979). Hendrix et. al (1985) found that family relationship had indirect effects on job stress through their impact on life stress. Crouter (1984) in a study noted that female employees with young children were "at risk" and experienced negative spillover from family responsibility to work, as reflected in tardiness and absenteeism, inattention and inefficiency, and inability to accept new responsibilities at work. Davidson and Cooper (1988) reported work–family interface to be a major source of stress for female managers and professionals. In a study, Srivastava and Krishna (1991) observed that females in "dual career couples" with part-time jobs experienced lesser role stress and maintained better mental health as compared to those who were in fulltime employment. Disturbed life patterns of miscellaneous stress (Neves, 1969), stressful life events (Dohrenwend & Dohrenwend, 1974), and demands of the husband and children of working women (Waldron, 1978) have been reported as off-the-job sources of occupational stress.

All the occupational stressors identified by stress researchers have been summarized below under two major categories, i.e., objectively defined and subjectively defined job stressors:

Objective Job Stressors

(*a*) Physical hazards, chronic dangers
(*b*) Pollution
(*c*) Noise
(*d*) Inadequate man-machine design
(*e*) Unusual/non-standard working hours
(*f*) Technical limitations
(*g*) Change in shift pattern.
(h) Deadlines
(*i*) Time pressure

Properties of Work and Work Setting

(*a*) New work setting
(*b*) Machine pacing
(*c*) Work overload
(*d*) Lack of training
(*e*) Inadequate intrinsic rewards
(*f*) Inadequate extrinsic rewards
(*g*) Poor management-labour relations
(*h*) Job insecurity
(*i*) Territoriality (alienation, isolation)
(*j*) Organizational structure
(*k*) Poor organizational climate
(*l*) Negative organizational attitude
(*m*) Inter-and intra-group competitions
(*n*) Job complexity.
(*o*) Qualitative worload
(*p*) Autocratic leadership
(*q*) Crowding
(*r*) Discrimination in resources and demand

Changes in Job

(*a*) Loss of job/employment

(*b*) Qualitative changes in job
(*c*) Overpromotion
(*d*) Transfer of job locus
(*e*) Null changes
(*f*) Job/career transition

Subjective Job Stressors

Occupational Role

(*a*) Role ambiguity
(*b*) Role conflict
(*c*) Less control over work processes
(*d*) Responsibility for people
(*e*) Responsibility for things
(*d*) Low participation
(*g*) Feedback and communication problems
(*h*) Self-role distance
(*i*) Role stagnation
(*j*) Resource inadequacy
(*k*) Role erosion
(*l*) Inter-role distance
(*m*) Role isolation

Miscellaneous

(*a*) Strained relationship with supervisor
(*b*) Inadequate support from supervisor
(*c*) Strained relationship with coworkers
(*d*) Conflict with subordinates
(*e*) Ambiguity about future
(*f*) Inequality of pay
(*g*) Quantity-quality conflict
(*h*) Building and maintaining career
(*i*) Lesser opportunity for advancement

Off-the Job Stressors

(*a*) Stressful life events
(*b*) Demands of husband and children
(*c*) Work-family conflicts
(*d*) Spillover effect of non-work stressors

3
CONSEQUENCES OF OCCUPTIONAL STRESS

Nature

Stress has been generally denoted as an undesirable and a negative force causing disruption in psychological and physiological homeostasis of the focal person. In a situation of severe stress, human constitution and capacities are taxed severely and his overall effectiveness is distorted. Majority of stress researchers have concluded that stress gives rise to negative emotional experiences causing significant deterioration in individuals' adjustment, behavioural effectiveness and health.

Consequences

The nature of the response to stress was first studied by Walter Cannon (1914) and in mid-1920s by Hans Selye. These two physiologists have made significant contribution to the understanding of stress response and the effects of its mismanagement. More recently there has been an important focus on the health consequences of stress in the workplace, both out of concern for individuals and organizations. This concern is founded on the idea that the intense or persistent stimulation of the stress response can result in a host of health problems. Researches in organizational stress have dominantly focused on emotional, behavioural and health outcomes of the stress experienced at work (Breif, Schuler, & Van Sell, 1981;

Cooper & Marshall, 1976; Ivancevich & Matteson, 1980). Thus we see that prolonged severe stress, affects the focal person at psychological as well as physiological levels. At mild level, stress may arouse the individual for improved performance and problem solving, but starts hampering performance when its intensity reaches a disruptive level, which varies with the characteristics of the focal person and the task being performed. Physiological consequences of stress include increase in serum and cholesterol levels, blood pressure, heart rate, adrenalin levels, and respiratory rates. With prolonged high level of stress a variety of psychosomatic diseases may occur. Various dimensions of job behaviour such as performance, job satisfaction, absenteeism and turnover are also affected by the stresses of job life. Schuler (1980) sub-merged all the consequences of job stress under three general categories: physiological, psychological and behavioural symptoms.

***Physiological Symptoms*:** Researches in health and medical sciences have concluded that stress could create changes in metabolism, increased heart and breathing rates, increased blood pressure, and bring on headaches, and induce heart attacks.

***Psychological Symptoms*:** Job related stress can cause job dissatisfaction, tension, anxiety, irritation, boredom, and procrastination.

***Behavioural Symptoms*:** Behaviourally related symptoms of stress include changes in productivity, absenteeism, and turnover, as well as changes in eating habits, increased smoking or consumption of alcohol and sleep disorders.

Reviewing the researches on the effects or products of occupational stress Holt (1982) enlisted its following consequences. He classified them as strains and illnesses.

Strains

Psychological Effects

(*a*) Job dissatisfaction
(*b*) Boredom, anxiety, depression irritation

(*c*) Low occupational and self-esteem
(*d*) Alienation from organization
(*e*) Tension, experienced conflict
(*f*) Fatigue
(*g*) Low satisfaction with life
(*h*) Sexual maladjustment

Behavioural and Social Effects

(*i*) Strikes
(*ii*) Early retirement
(*iii*) Burnout
(*iv*) High rate of smoking and caffine intake
(*v*) Use of drugs or alcohol on the job
(*vi*) Absenteeism
(*vii*) Disrupted performance of social roles
(*viii*) Interference with friendship and socializing
(*ix*) Accidents and errors
(*x*) Distortion in interpersonal relations.

Illness

Somatic-Physiological Effects

(*i*) Heart disease
(*ii*) Hyper-tension
(*iii*) Cerebral accident
(*vi*) Peptic ulcer
(*v*) Arthritis
(*vi*) Dermatitis, other skin afflictions
(*vii*) Diabetes

Psychological

(*i*) Mental illness
(*ii*) Depression
(*iii*) Neurotic symptoms
(*vi*) Mass psychogenic illness
(*v*) Suicide
(*vi*) Emotional outburst

For the present discussion, various consequences of occupational stress have been classified in two categories, namely, job-behavioural outcomes (i.e. job dissatisfaction, disruption in performance, high rate of absenteeism, and low level of job involvement) and health (somatic and mental) outcomes or strains.

Job-Behavioural Outcomes of Occupational Stress

Job Satisfaction: Job satisfaction is the most common and useful outcome measure of occupational stress. The stresses of job life develop negative attitudes about various aspects of the job in the focal employee which ultimately generate the feeling of job dissatisfaction in the employees. The relationship between job stress and job satisfaction was initially examined by Kahn and his associates (1964). They reported that job stress arising from role conflicts, role ambiguity, and role overload, result in a significant deterioration in job satisfaction of the focal employees. After the pioneering research of Kahn and his associates numerous studies have been made to examine the relationship between these two job variables. Rizzo, House, and Lirtzman (1970) in the samples of managers, engineers and office assistants and Tosi and Tosi (1970) in the sample of school teachers observed significant negative relationship between role stress (role conflict and role ambiguity) and job satisfaction. In several other studies also inverse relationship between role stress and job satisfaction was noted, however, role ambiguity was observed to be comparatively more effective in causing deterioration in job satisfaction of the employees. Keller (1975) noted that role conflict and role ambiguity were differently related to various dimensions of job satisfaction. Role conflict was negatively related with satisfaction with supervision, pay and promotion, but not with co-workers and work itself. Caplan, Cobb, and French (1975) reported that stresses arising from underutilization of skills and abilities, low participation in decision making, job insecurity, and poor social support from supervisors and co-workers cause dissatisfaction. Bedian and Armenakis (1981) conducted a path analytical study of the consequence of role conflict and role ambiguity. The analysis revealed that though role stress negatively relates to job satisfaction, the strength of the relationship lies through the path of interfering variables rather than through a direct relationship. Jagdish (1984) and Srivastava and Jagdish (1986) reported that stress arising from various aspects of job, such as role conflict, role ambiguity, role overload, underparticipation, intrinsic impoverishment, poor-peer relations, unprofitability, insecurity, group-pressures, supervisory style, etc., negatively correlate with employees' job satisfaction. Walshok (1981) examined the sex difference in the degree of negative relationship between job stress and satisfaction. The results indicated that women and men showed quite different levels of job satisfaction for the same jobs.

Occupational Stress and Performance

It is generally assumed and observed that there exists a negative relationship between stress and performance. But in fact, the effect of stress on performance varies with the degree of stress and the nature of the task performed. It has been empirically established that high level of job stress causes a deterioration in job performance (McGrath, 1976; Beehr & Newman, 1978). But at the same time it has also been reported that very low or no stress also associate with low performance level. In absence of stress the individual lacks arousal and so the motivation to perform. Hinkle (1973) has accordingly suggested that "to be alive is to be under stress." The best known and most thoroughly documented pattern in stress-performance literature is the inverted 'U' shaped relationship (McGrath 1976; Anderson, 1976; Keller, 1981). Moderate level of stress stimulates the body and increases its ability to react. In a situation of moderate stress individuals often perform their task better, more intensively or more rapidly. The curvilinear relationship between stress and performance can be traced back to the work of Yerks and Dodson (1908). Their model gained momentum with the development of Scott's (1966) activation theory of motivation, and at present it appears to be the most popular one (Allen, Hill, & Greer, 1982; Ivancevich & Matteson, 1981; Mc Lean, 1979; Meglino, 1977; and Moss, 1981). A number of laboratory experiments have also yielded inverted 'U' shaped relationship between stress and performance (Janis et al., 1969; Baddeley, 1972; Anderson, 1976; Kets de Vries 1979; and Cohen, 1980). In their study Srivastava and Krishna (1991) have also confirmed the inverted 'U' shaped relationship between job stress and performance.

in a sample of the technical personnel of a locomotive industry. Pestonjee and Singh (1987) also reported that job stress positively correlates with job satisfaction of the managers in private sector organizations.

Besides the degree of stress, certain kinds of stressors also have been noted to be functional to the performance. Hall and Lawler (1971) reported that job pressures involving time, financial responsibility and quality factors were related to positive organizational outcomes. Burke (1976) also observed that stress arising from excessive responsibility, large workload, making decisions that affect others were positively related to job satisfaction and so to the performance. Mathew (1986) has also advocated that particular types of stress are essential for being active.

However, consistent and severe stress of job life, necessarily cause noticeable deterioration in employee's performance (Kahn et al., 1965; McGrath, 1976; Beehr & Newman, 1978; Srivastava & Krishna, 1991). Too much stress places unattainable demands or constraints on a person, which results in lower performance. Even moderate level of stress can have negative influence on performance over the long term as the continued intensity of stress bears down the individual and saps his energy resources. Srivastava (1983) explored the relationship between role stress and performance (productivity), considering the latter as determinant of former than vice versa. The study revealed that employees, mentioning high productivity, experienced lesser stress by virtue of their productivity. It may also be noted here that nature of job being performed also determines the extent to which its performance and ensuing consequences would be affected by the felt stress. Jobs differ in such a way that a given level of stress might affect performance positively in one job and negatively in another. McGrath (1976) has postulated that stress-performance relationship would be of different nature in conditions when (i) task itself is a source of stress (e.g., a difficult or complicated task), (ii) the task is being performed under stressful conditions. In conditions where task is difficult, in relation to the capability of the focal person—then the more difficult (stressful) it is, the poorer would be the performance. There would be an inverse relationship between stress and performance effectiveness. In contrast, in second condition, when the task is being performed when other contextual stressors are operating, the availability of the task, as an attention and effort absorber, reduces the stressful effects of other stressful conditions. On the other hand, if the stress conditions operate so as to distract the focal person from the task, its presence would decrease performance effectiveness. This represents a very complex relationship, an interdependence between task performance and experienced stress rather than the usual assumption of a functional dependence of task performance and the level of stress.

Occupational Stress and Absenteeism and Turnover

Occupational stress has been observed to be associated with alienation and high rate of absenteeism and turnover of the employees. These job behaviours have been identified as symptoms of stress. (Akerstedt 1976; Schuler, 1980; Randall & Altmaier, 1984). However, substantial amount of research has not been made to examine the relationship between occupational stress and absenteeism and turnover. Though absenteeism and turnover represent attempts to cope with occupational stress, since both behaviours allow the employee to with draw from stressful situations, they cost a lot to the organization. These costs include the money it will take to recruit, select and train a new employee. Additional costs are seen in the decrease of productivity, as the raw employee replaces an experienced employee the costs incurred are interms of the increased amount of time it takes to supervise the new employee. Absenteeism affects not only productivity but it also serves to reduce an employees' level of motivation and thus exacerbate already existing problems (Matteson & Ivancevich, 1987). Despite the literature on turnover, there is little empirical data to support assertion that stress management programmes reduce job turnover (Murphy, 1985). In a recent study, Veena (1999) did not observe significant relationship between job stress and absenteeism.

Turnover and absenteeism are dependent criteria. Employees may show higher rate of absence before they actually leave. Turnover usually is a gradual process. People do not leave the jobs all of sudden, they begin to think about leaving and evaluate options before they quit. Turnover might also be determined by employees' assessment of their ability to find other jobs.

Occupational Stress and Accidents and Mortality

Accidents on the job have long been a subject of research, much of it is an inconclusive attempt to identify accident proneness. Though not empirically established, occupational stress is assumed to be associated with accident and mortality rates. There are no definite demonstrations that industrial accidents are caused by occupational stress, but enough positive indications from adequately complex research, warrant further careful study of accidents as the resultant of stressful conditions impinging upon dissatisfied employees. Accidents and errors, with harm to self (Theurell, 1974) and accidents causing harm to others (Colquhoum, 1976) have been noted to be caused by job stress. In some studies on air traffic control reviewed by Carump (1979) it was found that the relationship between occupational stress and consequent effects infer positive relationship between stress and accidents.

It has long been known that mortality rate differs across occupations (Cobb & Rose, 1973; Sales & House, 1971), indicating the vital significance of occupational stress. Research on death in general or as suicide, as dependent variable, is usually of a large scale. Studies of suicide rates by occupation and other demographic classifications have found that such stress-like or strain-like inferred variables of job life are weaknesses of social organizations and are significantly associated with self-destructive acts or attempts.

Occupational Stress and Job Involvement

Though job involvement is a relatively new concept, it has gained much importance because of its pivotal role of providing link between productivity and employees' needs and quality of working life. After the pioneering work of Lodhal and Kejner (1965) a good number of studies have been made by the researchers to explore the components, correlates and behavioural consequences of job involvement. During the last decade a substantial amount of research on the problem of job involvement has been carried out also by the psychologists in India. However, a very few attempts have been made to examine the relationship between job-related stress and job involvement. The attempts to empirically document the relationship between the two variables were initiated in the 1970s with modest success (Hanmer & Tosi, 1974; Beehr, Walsh, & Taber, 1976; Madhu & Hargopal, 1976).

In the early stage, job involvement was considered as one of the components of job satisfaction. But the later researches established that job involvement is a separate and independent construct, though it is positively related with job satisfaction in most of the cases. A good number of studies have been made to examine the relationship between the two. Weissenberg and Gruenfeld (1968) examined the relationship between job involvement and job satisfaction. The results of the investigation indicated a positive relationship between the two. Lawler and Hall (1970) and Cumming and Bigelow (1976) also reported positive correlation between job involvement and job satisfaction.

Since the job stress experienced by an employee is a product of interaction between environmental (job) and personal (employee) characteristics, employees' job attitudes and job involvement are very likely to interact with their occupational stress. Though not so many, some studies have been made by organizational psychologists in India and abroad to explore the relationship between job involvement and job stress. Tosi and Tosi (1974) investigated the relationship between role conflict and role ambiguity and various measures of job involvement in a sample of high level managers. The study yielded negative correlation between role ambiguity and role conflict and the measures of job involvement. It was also suggested that organizational level be taken into account when studying the relationship between these two variables. In another study Beehr, Walsh and Taber (1976) examined the effect of role stress on individually and organizationally valued stress. The results indicated that role overload was positively correlated with job involvement and other organizationally valued outcomes. Two other role stressors (i.e. role conflict and role ambiguity) were found to put adverse effects on both individually and organizationally valued outcomes including job involvement. It was also noted that the relationship between role stress and individually valued outcomes were moderated by high order need strength.

Among Indian researchers Madhu and Hargopal (1976) and Hargopal and Ravi Kumar (1979b) examined the relationship of stress stemming from role conflict and role ambiguity with job involvement. The investigations revealed significant negative relationship between role stress and job involvement. In another study Hargopal (1980) examined the moderating effect of personality variables i.e., ego-strength, submissiveness and dominance) on the relationship of role stress and job involvement. The results indicated that role stress negatively correlated with job involvement of employees with high ego-strength. It was also noted that role conflict and role ambiguity negatively correlate with job involvement of the employees of dominant nature. But the relationship between the two variables was found to be positive for the submissive group of employees.

In another study, Srivastava and Sinha (1983) examined the effect of ego-strength and job involvement on the experience of role stress (i.e. role overload, role conflict and role ambiguity) in a sample of middle management personnel. The results of the study indicated that high level of ego-strength and job involvement mitigate the employees' role stress arising from role overload and role ambiguity. Job involvement was found to be significantly negatively correlated with role overload and role ambiguity, but not with role conflict. Abel-Halim and Ahmad (1982) examined the moderating effect of social support on the relation of role stress with intrinsic job satisfaction and job involvement. The results indicated that there exists a negative relationship between role stress and job involvement. It was also noted that social support markedly moderates the adverse effect of role stress on job involvement.

In an extensive study Srivastava (1990) examined the

relationship between occupational stress and job involvement of the employees operating in public and private sector organizations. Employees' occupational stress was assessed through Occupational Stress Index (Srivastava & Singh, 1981), while the extent of their involvement in the job was estimated by employing Job Involvement Scale (Agrawal, 1978). The questionnaire comprise 32 items relating to 12 factors, namely, job longing, work underload, emotional involvement, persistence, energy expenditure, planfullness, task completion sensitivity, responsiveness to extra work, job devotion, job saliency, job concern and time-consciousness. The results of the study are recorded in Tables 3.1, 3.2 and 3.3.

Table 3.1
Correlation Between Occupational Stress and job Involvement

Occupational Stressors	*Public Sector Employees* (N=450)	*Private Sector Employees* (N=450)
Role overload	-.19**	-.06
Role ambiguity	-.30**	-.05
Role conflict	-.17**	-.01
Group pressures	-.27**	-.09
Responsibility for persons	-.11*	-.04
Underparticipation	-.17**	-.03
Powerlessness	-.21**	-.01
Poor peer-relations	-.21**	-.02
Intrinsic impoverishment	-.24**	-.01
Low status	-.20**	-.00
Stren. Work condition	-.24**	-.01
Unprofitability	-.19**	-.02
Overall Occupational Stress	-.37**	-.03

** $P < .01$;
** $P < .05$

The results recorded in Table 3.1 make it apparent that all the twelve dimensions of occupational stress negatively correlate with job involvement of the employees in public sector organizations. The results also specified that stress caused by role ambiguity correlate (negatively) most intensively to job involvement of the employees in public sector organizations. On the other hand, no significant correlation could be found between occupational stress and job involvement of the employees belonging to private sector organizations. The results enable us to conclude that employees' job involvement remains unaffected of their perceived job stress in private sector organizations.

After examining the correlation between occupational stress and job involvement of the employees operating in public and private sector organizations, stepwise multiple regression analysis was done to ascertain the potentiality of each occupational stressor in predicting job involvement of the employees. The obtained results are presented in Tables 3.2 and 3.3.

Table 3.2
Variance in Employees' Job Involvement Predicted by Occupational Stressors in Public Sector Organization

Occupational Stressors	*Job Involvement*		
	R	R^2	F
Role ambiguity	.299	.089	43.825**
Intrinsic impoverishment	.355	.126	32.325**
Powerlessness	.371	.137	23.662**
Unprofitability	.379	.144	18.687**
Poor peer-relations	.386	.149	15.590**
Grp. Pressures	.390	.152	13.233**
Stren. work conditions	.392	.154	11.480**
Respon. for persons	.394	.155	10.106**
Role conflict	.394	.155	8.983**
Role overload	.394	.155	8.072**

** $P < .01$.

The results (Table 3.2) indicate that all dimensions of occupational stress, excepting low status and under participation, predicted significant variance in job involvement of the employees of public sector organization. The analysis also revealed that the stress arising from role ambiguity caused maximum variance in employees' job involvement whereas the stress of role overload caused least variance in job involvement of these employees. The results also indicate that all the potential job stressors jointly caused a variance of 15.50 per cent in the job involvement of the employees in public sector organization. On the other hand, job related stressors were found to be comparatively ineffective in causing noticeable variance in job involvement of the private sector employees. (Table 3.3).

Table 3.3
Variance in Job Involvement Predicted by Occupational Stressors in Private Sector Organizations

Occupational Stressors	*Job Involvement*		
	R	R^2	F
Grp. pressures	.083	.007	3.283**
Stren. work conditions	.103	.011	2.418**
Respon. for persons	.112	.012	1.873
Role overload	.120	.014	1.623
Role conflict	.129	.017	1.302
Role ambiguity	.133	.018	1.326
Under participation	.136	0.19	1.181
Powerlessness	.142	.020	1.129
Poor peer-relation	.143	0.21	1.024
Intrinsic impoverishment	.144	.021	0.930
Low status	.144	0.21	0.84

The obtained results indicate that job stress arising only from group pressures and strenuous working conditions predicted significant variance in job involvement of the employees of private sector organizations.

Occupational Stress and Organizational Effectiveness

Occupational stress affects not only different aspects of job behaviour of the individual employees, but also ultimately results in a noticeable deterioration in overall effectiveness of the organization. Beehr (1978) suggested that it would be more fruitful to study the effect of stress on both the individual and the organization simultaneously and diachronically. Allen, Hitt and Greer (1982) noted in their study a negative relationship between stress and perceived organizational effectiveness. The results suggest that type of stress moderates the stress-effectiveness relationship. Dysfunctional job stress provided a better explanation of variations in effectiveness levels than total job stress levels. In another study, Srivastava and Benerjee (1990) found significant negative relationship between role stress and various dimensions of perceived organizational effectiveness, assessed through Organizatidnal Effectiveness Scale (Srivastava, 1997). The following Table (3.4) depicts the obtained results.

Table 3.4
Correlation Between Role Stress and Organizational Effectiveness

Dimensions of O.E.	*Organizational Role Stress*
Efficient organizational system	.176**
Congenial climate	.134**
Efficiency	.179**
Dynamism & adaptability	.101**
Interpersonal harmony	.144**
Effective leadership	.146**
High morale	.134**
Job satisfaction and commitment	.147**
Overall O.E.	.189**

** P.01

Health-Outcomes of Occupational Stress

One of the most important reasons the stress has generated so much of interest is that stress is involved in the etiology of both somatic and psychological illness. It has been largely accepted by stress researchers that high and consistent stress is unpleasant and dysfunctional, and causes significant deterioration in physical and psychological well being of the focal persons. Last couple of decades have witnessed considerable research attention devoted to the field of emotional and environmental stress as they relate to a wide variety of pathologies.

Occupational Stress and Physical Health

The relationship between mind and body has fascinated philosophers and scientists throughout history. It was believed that a person's mental state and physical activities were parts of the individual as a whole. The prevailing cultural model defining the relationship of body to consciousness tends to be reflected in the model of diseases. Consciousness, feelings, and thoughts have been conceived of as an epiphenamenon of physical process. Three hypothetical constructs formed the foundation of psychosomatic diseases and medicine. Presently, existing research in psycho-immunology, neuroendocrinology, neurophysiology is encouraging stress researchers to take new a look at the mind-body relationship, particularly at the issue of how psychological stress causes pathological changes in body function which, if intense or chronic, lead to various types of somatic diseases. Selye's (1966, 1983) elucidation of the body's response to stress has led to a better understanding of the biochemical anatomic, and neurohormonal changes that accompany adaptation to stress.

Though brain itself identifies threats, activities altering appraisals, and coping processes, and integrates body reactions with feeling, all parts of the body experience a major stress response. Following regions are particularly vulnerable to be affected by the experience of stress (Zegans, 1982):

(a) Hypothalamic-pitutary-endocrine axis
(b) Autonomic nervous system - adrenal medulla
(c) Immune system
(d) Reticular activating system
(e) Involuntary and strained muscle system
(f) Cognitive - affective integrating centres of the brain

By engaging the integrative system, stress can cause disease by:

(a) lowering the immune response,
(b) creating endocrine problems through hyperactivity or hypo-activity,

(c) altering the balance of autonomic control, resulting in changes in cardiovascular, respiratory secretory, and visceral system,
(d) altering sleep patterns with attendant impact on protein metabolism, harmone secretion, and other vegetation functions,
(e) changes in peptide release in extra CNS. sites,
(f) affecting neurotransmitter, neuromodulator, and neuro endocrine functions of the brain.

Rahe and his associates (1964), Rahe (1968), Holmes and Rahe (1967) examined whether changes in individual's life, which require them to make behavioural readjustments, statistically correlate with the onset of illness. The psychophysiological studies indicate that naturally occurring and experimentally induced stress evoke significant alternations in the functioning of most bodily tissues, organs and systems. These changes in their turn lead to a lowering of the body's resistance to diseases by suppressing the immune system. The greater the magnitude of such life events, the greater is the risk of acquiring illness of a serious nature has been reported by a number of investigators (Rahe et. al., 1964; Holmes & Rahe, 1967; Insel & Moss, 1974; Maddi et. al., 1987; Lai, 1995; Srivastava & Pestonjee, 1997).

Substantial amount of research has been done by psychologists to examine health (somatic) outcomes of occupational stress. Majority of these investigations have revealed positive relationship between job related stress and a variety of somatic symptoms and disorders. In view of the severity of stress-outcomes, Halt (1982) has classified them in two categories: (i) physiological strains relatively minor side effects of occupational stresses, (ii) illness and mortality impairing effect of occupational stresses on health causing illnesses. Reviewing these studies, Holt (1982) has enlisted following strains and illnesses and mortality observed correlated with occupational stress.

Physiological Strains

(i) High pulse rate and blood pressure (Caplan, 1975)
(ii) High serum cholesterol, high and low-density leproteins (Chadwiek, 1980)

(iii) High serum cholesterol, thyroid hormones, serum uric acid (Caplan et al., 1975)
(iv) Catacholamine excretion (Fronkenhaeuser and Gardell, 1976)
(v) High electrocardiogram (Serum et al., 1973)
(vi) Disrupted sleep, bowel function, eating habits. (Mott, 1976)
(vii) Somatic complaints (Caplan, et al., 1975)

Illnesses and Mortality

(i) Heart disease (Glass, 1977)
(ii) Hypertension (Cobb & Rose, 1973)
(iii) Cerebral stroke (Work in America, 1973)
(iv) Peptic ulcer (Cobb & Rose, 1973; House et al., 1979)
(v) Arthritis (Cobb, 1971)
(vi) Headache (Kimball, 1979)
(vii) Respiratory illness (Caplan et al., 1975)
(viii) Dermatitis, other skin afflictions (House et al., 1979)
(ix) Diabetes melitus (Cobb & Rose, 1973)
(x) General diffuse sickness (Mechanic, 1974)
(xi) Total rate of illness (Hinkle, 1974; Rahe et al., 1974)
(xii) Mortality rates (Colligan et al., 1977).

One of the most common and fatal resultants of occupational stress are coronary heart diseases. Growing body of evidence indicate that perhaps one half of all the cardiac deaths result not from blockage of coronary arteries, as it is the case of heart attack, but from the condition known as "sudden cardiac death", in which death is believed to result from sudden and serious cardiac rhythm disturbances. In organizational set-up the study on the relationship between stresses of job life and coronary heart disease (CHD) was initiated by Caplan (1971). Further, extensive studies were done to examine the relationship between the two in context of some other variables such as personality type, social support, work motivation, etc. (French & Caplan, 1972; House, 1972; Sherom et al., 1973; Caplan et al., 1975; House et al., 1976; Eden et al., 1977; Kaufman, & Beehr, 1989; Levy, 1989; Jamal, 1990). In these studies a positive relationship was observed between severe occupational stress and risk for CHD. It was also revealed that the relationship between stress and risk for CHD is moderated by personality type, work motivation of the focal person, and the social support perceived by him while in the situation of stress. In a study Srivastava (1997) noted that job stress was significantly associated with psychosomatic health complaints and pathogenic health habits. In some other studies by Indian researchers positive relationship was noted between job stress and physical illnesses among police personnel (Pillai, 1987; Ramchandran, 1989). However, this problem has not been extensively studied by organizational psychologists in India.

Even cancer has been reported to be associated with stress. In western countries about 75 per cent of lung cancer are attributed to smoking. To the extent that organizational stress increases smoking behaviour, it will increase lung cancer and other tobacco-related cancers such as bladder cancer, stomach cancer, and cancer of the mouth, throat and lungs. Literature on stress and cancer provides evidence suggesting that stressful events are associated with appearance of a variety of cancers, including breast cancer, uterine cancer, and lung cancer (Tache et al., 1979; Cooper, 1984). Stress appears to have a direct effect on decreasing the immune response which might otherwise control a small cancer (McClelland, 1985).

Occupational Stress and Mortality

Numerous strides reviewed by different stress researchers have associated work overload, job dissatisfaction, job insecurity, role conflict, interpersonal strains and variety of other work stresses with classic symptoms of stress such as headache, heart-burn and generalized fatigue (Quick and Quicks) 1984 Table 3.5 is a summary of the information on ten leading causes of mortality in USA in a year. Although genetic, biological development, and many other factors influence the appearance and course of these conditions, there is a growing body of empirical findings suggesting that job stress plays a role in hardening the appearance of diseases.

Table 3.5
Ten Leading Causes of Mortality in USA

Cause of Death	*Number of Deaths*	*Reference*
Heart disease	975,660	Frasure-Swith & Prince (1985)
Cancer	459,200	Fanch & Marshall (1983)
Stroke	153,330	Julius (1984)
Accidents and adverse effects	91,690	Jones (1984)
Chronic obstructive lung disease	73,430	Schilling et al (1985)
Pneumonia and influenza	65,230	Locke et al (1984)
Diabetes	27,350	Kisch (1985)
Suicide	27,350	Karcher & Linden (1982)
Liver cirrhosis	26,740	Trell et al (1985)
Homicide	19,310	Steadmon & Ribner (1982)

Occupational Stress And Mental Health

Mental Health: Health is, undoubtedly, an indispensible quality in a human being. It has been described as the soil from which the finest flowers grow. Therefore, neglecting one's health for other virtues in life is said to be the greatest of follies. The growth of science, technology, and materialistic predominance, and hazards and complexities of social life have caused a marked deterioration in mental health of the people in modern societies. Most of the medical scientists and psychologists have been dealing with diseases or illness rather than health, therefore, the phenomenon of 'health' remained neglected. But during the past few decades medical as well as behavioural scientists realized the importance of health.

Mental health covers an elusive and diffused field, and the term itself encompasses a multiplicity of meanings. The concept of mental health has been vaguely defined by psychologists and psychiatrists. It is very difficult to determine the cut point of mental health and mental illness. Ionesco (1960) has accordingly expressed that "...... who can say where the normal stops and the abnormal starts". However, attempts have been made to define mental health, and to some extent satisfactory conclusions have been drawn by the researchers. Before the second half of the twentieth century, mental health was considered as the absence of mental disease. But it is interesting to note that the concept of mental disease also has not its adequate definition. In such a situation, definition of one vague concept in terms of the absence of another ambiguous concept may not provide a satisfactory meaning of the concept. Therefore, since the second half of the twentieth century mental health and mental illness have been characterized as sharply disparate and it was suggested that the absence of ill-health may constitute a necessary but not satisfactory definition of mental health. As a consequence, mental health has been considered in its more positive connotation, not as the absence of mental illness. Conrad (1952) attempted to differentiate the positive health from non-health and negative health. To her, "positive health consists in ways of living that are beyond the frontiers of more social existence implied by negative health. This category (positive health) applies when there is evidence that the individual fully utilizes a capacity or is working in that direction".

A qualitative distinction between mental health and mental illness has also been established by some psychologists and psychiatrists. Rumke (1955) was of the view that "the understanding of the disturbances of a sick man hardly contributes to the understanding of normal man". Thus, proper definition of mental health may not be given as mere absence of mental diseases. Positive connotation of mental health must be kept in mind to understand the human personality. Several psychiatrists and behavioural scientists have presented their views about the nature of psychological health in various ways. Maslow and Mittelman (1951) have suggested the following criteria for normal psychological health:

(i) Adequate feeling of security;
(ii) Adequate self-evaluation;
(iii) Adequate spontaneity and emotionality;
(iv) Efficient contact with reality;
(v) Adequate self-knowledge;
(vi) Integration and consistency of personality;
(vii) Adequate life goals;
(viii) Ability to learn from experience;
(ix) Ability to satisfy the requirements of the groups;
(x) Adequate anticipation from the group or culture.

Reviewing the psychological literature on mental health, Jahoda (1958) has noted six aspects of positive mental health, such as attitudes of an individual toward his own self; growth, development or self-actualization; integration; autonomy; perception of reality; and environmental mastery. Kornhauser (1965) described mental health of workers as "those behaviours, attitudes, perceptions, and feelings that determine a worker's overall level of personal effectiveness, success, happiness, and excellence of functioning as a person". Schultz (1977) has noted seven criteria of sound mental health, i.e., extension of the sense of self, warm relation of self to others, emotional security, realistic perception, skills and assignments, self-objectification, and a unifying philosophy of life. Evaluating major models of healthy personality, Schultz has drawn following conclusions: there is no single prescription for or description of psychological health on which all psychologists or personality theorists would agree. Perhaps the only point on which most of the theorists agree fully is that "psychologically healthy persons are in conscious control of their lives".

***Occupational Stress and Mental Health*:** Social contexts such as low social and occupational status have long been associated with increased risk of nearly all disease conditions and with shorter life expectancy. Specific conditions such as personal loss, bereavement, job loss and conditions of marital status and mobility are similarly associated with risk of illness. Though the belief that stressful life events cause mental disorders is of long standing, empirical research involving acceptable methodology into the issue is more recent. The stress generated from inadequacies of various aspects of job life and its on-the-job as well off-the-job consequences have largely attracted the interest of organizational psychologists and management scientists. A substantial amount of research, using acceptable methodology, has been conducted to identify various sources of occupational stress and to examine the consequences of occupational stress. The researches in this area have revealed that consistent stress at work does not only affect employees' job behaviour and job attitudes, but also deteriorates mental as well as physical health of the focal employees.

Kornhauser (1965) draw the attention of psychologists toward the stress prevailing in work environment and its impairing effect on mental health of the employees. He reported that unpleasant work conditions, necessity to work fast, expenditure of large physical efforts, and excessive and inconvenient hours of work lead to poor mental health of the employees. But a systematic attempt to ascertain the psychological consequences of organizational stress was initiated by Kahn et al. (1964). In their extensive study they analyzed the effect of different organizational role stresses on the behaviour of focal employees. Thereafter, innumerous studies were made to examine the effect role stress and various organizational and occupational variables on mental health of the employees.

Role Stress and Mental Health: Job role of an employee is the most potential source of his satisfaction as well as frustration and stress, which he experiences at work. Inadequacies in job role and constraints and hindrances in its enactment have been recognized as a frequent cause of stress in the organization leading to a deterioration in the psychological well being of the focal employees. Kahn and his associates were first to systematically analyze the different kinds of role stress and its organizational and psychological consequences. These researchers concluded that stress resulted from role conflict and role ambiguity leads to low self-confidence, greater futility and high job-related tension. French and Caplan (1970), out of their study, noted that role ambiguity was significantly correlated with the feeling of job related threat, and mental and physical health of the employees. In another study, role conflict was observed to be positively correlated with threat and high anxiety (Tosi & Tosi, 1970; Rizzo and his associates, 1970) noted a positive relationship between role stress and anxiety, tension and fatigue. In a study of working women, Hall and Gorden (1973) found that role conflict leads to the feeling of unhappiness. Margolis, Kore and Quinn (1974) reported that role ambiguity significantly correlates with various indicators of physical and mental ill-health. Stress caused from role conflict was reported to be positively correlated with threat, anxiety and tension (Hanmer & Tosi 1974; Miles, 1975; Brief & Aldag, 1976). In further studies, role ambiguity was found to be correlated with low self-esteem (Caplan & Jone, 1975; Beehr, 1976). Gavin and Axelrod (1979) documented positive relationship of role conflict with anxiety, depression and irritation among managers. Morris and Koch (1979) reported that role stresses were associated with psychiatric complaints. Christopher (1982), out of his study on middle managers, noted a significant positive correlation between role conflict and physical and psychological strains leading to a deterioration in psychological health. Organizational psychologists in India have also made some attempts to examine the relationship between role stress and employees' mental health. In a study Srivastava (1983) examined the relationship of role stress and mental ill-health in a sample of white-collar employees. The study revealed that stress arising from role ambiguity and role conflict positively correlates with various symptoms of neuroticism, such as free-floating anxiety, obsessive compulsive neurosis, phobic neurosis, neurotic depression, and somatic concomitants of anxiety. In two studies of Srivastava (1985) and Srivastava and Srivastava (1986), significant correlation was observed between role stress (role ambiguity and role conflict) and mental ill-health in a sample of two-career couples. The results also indicated that husbands in two-career couples experienced more role stress and manifested more symptoms of mental ill-health. In another study aimed at examining the moderating effect of coping strategies on the relationship of organizational role stress and mental health, Srivastava and Singh (1988) noted positive relationship between role stress and ill-health. The study also revealed that approach coping strategies attenuates the adverse effects of role stress on mental health to a noticeable extent. Srivastava and Jagdish (1989) reported that stress arising from role conflict was most intensively correlated (negatively) with psychological well being of the supervisory personnel. In her extensive study, Benerjea (1989) noted negative relationship between role stress and mental health of employees in service organizations. The investigation also documented that the stress resulted from inter-role distance caused maximum variance in psychological health of the non-manufacturing employees whereas, the stress arising from self-role distance predicated maximum variance in psychological well being of the employees belonging to manufacturing organizations.

Employees' mental health has also been studied in relation to the stress generated from role overload. Out of their investigation French, Tuper, and Mueller (1965) concluded that qualitative work overload experienced by the university professors was significantly correlated with low self-esteem. Terryberry (1988) reported that overload in most systems leads to breakdown, whether we deal with single biological cell or individuals in an organization. Gavin and Axelrod (1977) have noted that work overload produces high anxiety and irritation among the focal employees. Martin (1984) in his investigation concluded that role overload predicated acute and chronic mental problems. Rod and Herbert (1984) reported role overload to have a replicable positive relationship with mental health problems. Cooper and Roden (1985) in their study on a sample of tax officers noted that qualitative and quantitative work overload was a major cause of poor psychological health of the subjects. Inverse relationship between stress of role overload and psychological well being was observed by Jagdish and Srivastava (1989) in their study on a sample of technical supervisors.

Other Job Stressors and Mental Health

Besides the role stress, the effect of stress arising from several other organizational and occupational variables on employees' mental health has also been examined by the stress researchers. In a study Arther and Gunderson (1965) found that stress resulted from promotional lag was relate to psychiatric disorders. Brook (1973) reported that both over promotion and under promotion were associated with mental illness. Quinn, Seashore, and Mangione (1971) reported that close supervision and lack of autonomy at work was positively correlated with employees' poor mental health. Buck (1972) noted that workers who felt that their boss was low on consideration reported the feeling of more job pressure leading to poor mental health. In another study, status-congruency was found to be negatively related to the incidences of psychiatric disorders (Erikson, Edwards, & Gunderson, 1973). Bures and Buresova (1974) reported that subjects under stressful conditions exhibit aggression, withdrawal and reflective responses. Gardell (1975) in his study concluded that workers whose jobs were severely circumscribed in two job contents, i.e., the degree of direction given to the workers to maintain pace and working method, and the possibility of using a variety of human resources in the performance of work, react with strain and feeling of monotony and manifest symptoms of impaired mental health. Gavin and Axelrod (1977) reported that employees who perceived the work environment as having well defined organizational structure, minimal interference in work procedure, equitable reward system, and an atmosphere of trust and consideration scored higher on the measures of sound mental health. On the other hand, job stresses, such as under utilization of skills, job insecurity, variation in work load, lack of participation were noted to produce high anxiety, depression and irritation in the focal employees. Martin (1984) reported that employee's inability to leave his job resulted in acute and chronic mental health problems. Stout (1984) examined employees' stress and health problems in relation to supervisory orientations. The study revealed that the employees whose supervisore exhibited high structured (stress) and low considerate behaviour were found to have comparatively more health problems. Agervold (1985) reported that there was a strong link between stressful physical work environment and health problems. It was also noted that mental exhaustion increased with a greater work pace and greater work difficulty.

Furham & Schaeffer (1984) examined the consequences of person-environment incongruence at work. The stress arising form misfit between the employees and his job demands has been reported to cause deterioration in their mental health. Harrison (1976) and French et al. (1982) observed positive relationship between P-E misfit and psychological strain and somatic complaints.

In their extensive study House and his associates (1979) found that perceived job stress was consistently correlated with self-reported angina, ulcer and neurotic symptoms, and with hypertension and other heart disease risk factors. Kobasa (1982) noted significant relationship between experienced job stress and complaints of strain symptomology. Syrotuik and Arey (1983) analyzed health-related consequences of occupational stress. The study revealed that occupational stress was related to job strains, general ill-health, and alcohol consumption. In a study on the sample of school teachers Gallowy (1984) found high correlation between occupational stress and mental ill-health. Revieki and May (1985) reported that occupational stress exerted a direct effect on depression of the employees. In a study on a large sample of blue-collar workers, Frese (1985) noted that objective conditions of work stress influenced the development of subjective stress and psychosomatic complaints. In their extensive study, Jagdish and Srivastava (1989) noted that occupational stress generated from various inadequacies and constraints of job life negatively correlated with psychological well being of the employees. The results also indicated that stress resulted from "intrinsic impoverishment" was one of the most potential causes of deterioration in employees' psychological health.

In an extensive study, Srivastava (1990) examined the relationship between occupational stress and mental health in two separate samples of the employees of public and private sector organizations. Besides the relationship between job stress and health, the study revealed the moderating effect of the nature of the organization on the relationship of the two. The extent of employees' job stress arising from twelve aspects of job was assessed through Occupational Stress Index (Srivastava & Singh, 1981). Mental health of the employees was estimated on the basis of the severity of the symptoms of psychoneurotic patterns manifested by the employees. The severity of the symptoms of six psychoneurotic patterns, namely, free-floating anxiety, obsessive compulsive neurosis, fobic neurosis, neurotic depression, somatic concomitants of anxiety, and hysteria neurosis was assessed by employing Indian adaptation (Srivastava & Bhatt, 1973) of the Middlesex Hospital Questionnaire (Crown & Grisp, 1966). The correlational analysis of occupational stress and mental ill-health of the public sector employees revealed significant positive relationship between all the dimensions of occupational stress, excepting the stress of "responsibility of persons" and various symptoms of mental ill-health. The obtained coefficients of correlation indicate that overall occupational stress experienced by the public sector employees explains 17.64 per cent variance in their mental ill-health. The results also indicate that employees' occupational stress caused maximum variances in their symptoms of free-floating anxiety, phobic neurosis and neurotic depression. The analysis also revealed that employees' stress arising from unsatisfactory monetary gains and benefits accounts for maximum variance (10.24 per cent in their mental ill-health followed by the stress arising from the feeling of powerlessness (8.31 per cent) (Table 3.6).

Table 3.6
Coefficient of Correlation Between Occupational Stress and Mental Ill-Health of the Employees in Public Sector Organization (N=450).

Occupational Stressors	*Mental Ill-Health (Neurotic Patterns)* FFA	OCN	FN	ND	SCA	HN	*Overall M/I-H*
Role overload	.16**	.11*	.18**	.13**	.19**	.14**	.21**
Role conflict	.25**	.19**	.26**	.21**	.24**	.23**	.23**
Role ambiguity	.21**	.17**	.20**	.18**	.19**	.18**	.26**
Grp. pressures	.20**	.11*	.16**	.23**	.23**	.19**	.26**
Resp. for persons	.09	.08	.04	.03	.09	.09	.08
Underparticipation	.15**	.09	.14**	.24**	.18**	.20**	.23**
Powerlessness	.20**	.19**	.21**	.20**	.23**	.22**	.29**
Poor peer-relation	.13**	.15**	.16**	.15**	.15**	.15**	.21**
Intrinsic impoverishment	.20**	.19**	.15**	.11*	.18**	.19**	.24**
Low status	.15**	.19**	.24**	.08	.10*	.13**	.21**
Strenuous work cond.	.18**	.18**	.22**	.07	.12*	.15**	.22**
Unprofitability	.24**	.20**	.26**	.23**	.25**	.22**	.31**
Overall Occupl. Stress	.32**	.27**	.32**	.28**	.32**	.31**	.41**

* P < .05
**P < .01

Table 3.7

Coefficient of Correlation Between Occupational Stress and Mental Ill-Health of the Employees of Private Sector Organization (N=450).

Occupational Stressors	*Mental Ill-Health (Neurotic Patterns)* FFA	OCN	PN	ND	SCA	HN	*Overall* M/I-H
Role overload	.02	.17**	.05	.07	.05	.07	.11*
Role conflict	.12*	.08	.08	.08	.06	.11**	.12*
Role ambiguity	.11*	.50	.10*	-.05	.05	.10*	.11*
Grp. pressures	.08	.50	.04	.09	.07	.08	.09
Resp. for persons	-.02	-.04	.09	-07	-06	.00	.09
Underparticipation	.00	-.04	.06	.03	.03	.01	.02
Powerlessness	-.02	-.07	.07	.07	.02	-.01	-.01
Poor peer-relations	.02	.04	-.01	.05	-.01	.08	.04
Intrinsic impoverish.	.12*	.11*	.14**	.12*	.07	.18**	.17**
Low status	.12*	.06	.13**	.10*	.10*	.14**	.15**
Stren. work cond.	.08	.00	.01	.09	.06	.12*	.08
Unprofitability	.01	-.09	-.01	.00	.06	.05	.00
Overall Occupl. Stress	.01*	.07	.09	.11*	.08	.14**	.14**

* P < .05

** P < .01

But the picture of correlation between job stress and mental health of the employees in private sector organizations is quite different. The results indicate that the stress experienced by the employees in this sector is not so effective in deteriorating their mental health, as it is in case of the public sector employees (Table 3.7). Stress arising only from role overload, role ambiguity, role conflict, intrinsic impoverishment, and low status have been found to be significantly correlated with overall mental ill-health of the employees. It was also noted that the stress arising from the feeling of intrinsic impoverishment correlates most intensively with mental ill-health of these employees. An overall picture of the relationship between occupational stress and mental ill-health of the employees in two sectors enables us to conclude that the relationship between the two variables is comparatively more intensive for the public sector employees than employees for the private sector. The results also indicate that intensity of positive relationship of stress stemming from role ambiguity, role conflict, group pressures, under participation, powerlessness, poor peer-relations, strenuous working conditions and low-profitability with mental ill-health are significantly higher for the employees in public sector organizations than for private sector employees.

Stepwise multiple regression analysis was also run to ascertain the potentiality of various job stressors in predicting mentall Ill-health of the employees. The obtained results are recorded in the following Tables (3.8 and 3.9).

Table 3.8
Variance in Employees' Mental Ill-Health Predicted by Occupational Stressors in Public Sector Organizations (N = 450)

Occupational Stressors	*Mental Ill-Health (Neurotic Symptoms)*		
	R	R^2	*F*
Unprofitability	.322	.104	51.841**
Role ambiguity	.387	.150	39.432**
Powerlessness	.433	.187	34.233**
Role conflict	.449	.202	28.125 **
Intrin, impoverishment	.457	.229	23.418**
Poor peer-relations	.460	.211	19.777**
Stren. work conditions	.461	.213	17.072**
Under participation	.462	.213	14.955**
Low status	.462	.214	13.293**
Grp. pressures	.463	.214	11.968**
Respon. for persons	.463	.214	10.862

**P < .01

Table 3.9
Variance in Employees' Mental Ill-Health Predicted by Occupational Stressors in Public Sector Organizations (N = 450)

Occupational Stressors	*Mental Ill-Health (Neurotic Symptoms)*		
	R	R^2	*F*
Intrin. Impoverish-ment	.173	.030	13.794**
Low status	.191	.037	8.485**
Role overload	.204	.042	6.440**
Unprofitability	.215	.046	5.385**
Underparticipation	.224	.050	4.713**
Respon. for persons	.237	.056	4.388**
Powerlessness	.243	.059	3.956**
Poor peer-relations	.246	.060	3.547**
Grp. pressures	.249	.062	3.232**
Stren. work condition	.249	.062	2.004**
Role ambiguity	.249	.062	2.635**

* $P < .01$

On the other hand, in case the private sector employees, all the job stressors, excepting role conflict, were found to put significant effect on their mental health. However, the amount of variance in mental ill-health caused by job stress was very little (i.e. 6.20 per cent). It was also observed that the stress arising from intrinsic impoverishment and role ambiguity were, respectively, most and least effective in causing variance in mental ill-health of the employees belonging to the private sector organizations.

Occupational Stress and Burnout

In the present times the term "burnout" has become a popular one, and is confused with the concept of occupational stress. However, burnout occurs as a result of chronic job stress (Pines and Aronson, 1981). It is one of the extreme consequences of consistent job stress. Burnout, in fact, has three parts, namely, physical, emotional, and mental. Physical exhaustion is one components of burnout. Individuals, who are burnt out report intense weariness, often combined with an inability to sleep. In addition, symptoms of low energy, chronic fatigue and weakness are common. The second part of burnout is emotional exhaustion. In this stage the burnt out employee manifests feelings of depression, helplessness and hopelessness. Satisfaction with job and life in general is reduced. The third part of burnout is mental exhaustion; the affected employee shows negative attitude towards work, clients and fellow-workers. There is a dehumanizing aspect of these attitudes, where burnt out workers fail to respond to the feelings of others. The negative attitude and dehumanizing tendency may spillover to family and friends. Paine (1982) argued that Burnout Stress Syndrome (BOSS) can lead to depletion of energy, lowered resistance to illness, increased dissatisfaction and pessimism, and increased absenteeism and inefficiency at work. Venigle and Spradly (1981) mentioned five stages of burnout, i.e., honeymoon stage, fuel shortage stage, chronic symptoms stage, crisis stage, and hitting wall stage.

Burnout has severe short-and long-term consequences. The burnt out employees may not only leave their jobs, but also their professions. The cost to society of leaving these well trained and experienced professionals is a high one. Other workers who remain in their jobs gradually loose enthusiasm and interest in their jobs and for their own personal and professional development. Such workers present particular challenges for intervention, since they grow unwillingness to accept a different job which might be more interesting or involving even when offered.

Positive Consequences of Job Stress

It has been a general observation that job stress by its nature is extremely aversive to most employees. It creates noxious situations in the work environment causing significant deterioration in effectiveness of the employees and of the organization. However, stress is not always undesirable and harmful. It has a positive value as well. Recognizing its positive value, Selye, taking from the Greek prefix, coined the term "eustress" for a positive stress.

Some researchers are of the opinion that without stress modern organizations would loose the name of action. It is argued that stress creates as well as promotes employee's inclination towards job, thus enhances his capacity to work. Hinkle (1973) has accordingly written that "to be alive is to be under stress". Some researchers have contended that some sort of job stress have functional qualities and others have reported that partial degree of stress is desirable to motivate the individual and at which his effectiveness is maximized. Kets de Vries (1979) has noted that each individual needs a moderate amount of stress to be alert and capable of functioning effectively in the organization. Anderson (1976) observed inverted 'U'-shaped relationship between stress and performance, which indicates that a moderate level of stress is optimal for performance, whereas low and high degree of stress cause deterioration in performance level. Other researchers have also noted curvilinear relationship between stress and performance (Baddely, 1972; Meglino, 1977; Cohen, 1980; Moss, 1981; Ivancevich & Matteson, 1981; Allen et al., 1982; Jamal, 1984; Srivastava and Krishna, 1991.

Besides the magnitude of stress, sources and imagined outcomes of the stress determine the effect of stress. The stress arising from certain job factors have been observed to put positive effect on job behaviour and well being of the employees. Hall and Lawler (1971) found that job pressures involving time, financial responsibility and quality factors were related to positive organizational outcomes. Burke (1976) also observed that job stress arising from excessive responsibility, perceiving oneself not qualified excessively large workload, and making decisions that affect the lives of others were positively related to job satisfaction. Burke (1976) denoted the stress arising from these factors as 'functional role stress'. Srivastava and Krishna (1991) in their measure of 'functional role stress' have included five role stressors having positive value, viz., responsibility for persons, excessive responsibility (with authority), taking decisions that affect others, strenuous tasks that bring recognition and facilitate personal growth, and perceiving oneself not fully competent.

Job stress has also been found to be positively related to

job satisfaction of the managers of private sector organizations (Pestonjee & Singh, 1967). Mathew (1986) has advocated that particular types of stresses are essential for being creative. In their study Srivastava and Singh (1987) noted positive relationship between stress arising from 'responsibility for persons' and psychological well being in a sample of Banking and Insurance supervisors.

Health Benefits of Stress

Though occupational stress has been labelled as harmful causing a variety of somatic disorders, certain components of stress have been found to be beneficial to the health of the focal person. Milsum (1984) has explored positive aspects of optimal or well-balanced stress. Recent evidences also indicate that stress can markedly increase blood level endorphins, naturally occurring morphine-like hormones associated with pain relief and feelings of well-being (McCubin, Surwit, & Williams, 1985). Increased secretion of pineal, in stress situation "melatonin", has been noted to play a role in promoting homeostasis and adaptation under adverse environmental conditions. It is also a possibility that melatonin secretion may modulate the effect of stress on other glands such as the adrenal gland (Johnson, 1981). It inhibits tumerogenesis and tumer growth (Tamarkin, et al., 1985) Melatonin may offer protection against mammary cancer through a suppressive effect on prolaction secretion or an action on oestrogen receptors.

There are three stressful activities which have been observed to be helpful in either of the three specific or general circumstances. The first of these is aerobic fitness. The benefits of aerobic fitness are primarily in improved cardiovascular activities. The benefits include lower heart rate, greater stroke volume, and decreased reactivity to stressful situations. It has also been noted that weights training designed to strengthen the body, a stressful activity, has specific benefits when it comes to extreme physical environment. (Aerospace Medicine Division, 1985). The third stressful activity of benefit is flexibility training. The improved flexibility enables improved body posture, a key issue in considering the physical stresses imposed on the body during the normal course of living.

4
MANAGEMENT OF OCCUPATIONAL STRESS

Though stress has become an inevitable part of people's life in present day world, it is not entirely uncontrollable and unmanageable. The individual cannot constantly remain in the state of stress, he certainly makes some sort of adaptive behaviour to cope with or get rid of the stressful situations. It might be fight or flee. Since their origin, the human beings have been encountering the situations of stress and using some remedies or strategies to cope with these situations. But these coping efforts were not well planned and systematic. In present era of stress nd anxiety, when the cost of stress has markedly increased, the stress researchers and practitioners have concentrated on evolving systematic techniques for the management of the stresses of life in general and of job life in particular. It has become a legitimate field of endeavour, and is evolving quickly. The field of stress management has progressed substantially after Lehrer and Woolfolk published first edition of *Principles and Practice of Stress Management* in 1984. Like the term 'psychotherapy' the term 'stress management' is a global concept and involves quite a mix of techniques. The term can be broken into a number of operational steps or phases. Stress management interventions have been differently classified by various stress researchers and practitioners. Some have classified them on the basis of the stages of the process of stress, while others have classified them on the basis of orientation or location of the intervention programmes, i.e., individual and work setting (Ross & Altmair, 1994). Some practitioners have classified them in two categories:

(*a*) individual interventions and

(*b*) group interventions;

while others have grouped them into cognitive, behavioural and physiological interventions. Mathney and his associates (1986) classified individual interventions for stress as: (a) preventive interventions response to alleviate stress as it is initially perceived, and (b) combative coping strategies for mitigating stressors already underway. In fact the preventive interventions include three types of strategies, i.e., psychological or cognitive, behavioural, and physiological. Murphy (1987) classified the approaches to the problem of stress management into three categories:

(i) organizational change (eliminating the sources of stress by altering features of the organisation or job tasks);

(ii) job (enrichment making the work activity more challenging and interesting),

(iii) individual centered techniques (educating workers to prevent or reduce distress).

Currently most of the writers on stress management refer to one of the following three forms of stress management practices:

1. Employees Assistance Programmes: This has provisions for employees counselling services by the organization (Murphy, 1988).

2. Stress Management Training (SMT): The SMT includes training courses designed to provide employees with skill for coping with their job stressors, including technique such as meditation, bio-feedback, stress reduction, (Newton, 1992).

3. Stress Reduction Interventions: It includes interventions designed to change the level or form of job stressor experienced by employees, usually through job redesigning or work reform.

For the present discussion different interventions, strategies and techniques of the management of occupational stress have been classified in five categories in an order of their operational stage. Though this categorization has been made on the basis of different stages of stress management, they are not absolutely separate from each other. Rather, they are interlinked in the form of different stages of a process with an ultimate objective to effectively manage the stresses of job life and the consequent strains. One category of stress management strategies may be combined with the strategies of other categories in order to achieve better results.

Stree Management strategies:

1. Prevention of occupational stress
   (a) At individual level
      (*i*) Cognitive intervention strategies
      (*ii*) Behavioural intervention strategies
      (*iii*) Physiological intervention strategies
   (b) At organizational level
2. Eliminating or mitigating organizational stressors
3. Coping with occupational stress
4. Moderating occupational stress and consequent strains
5. Therapeutic treatment of stress-disorders

Prevention of Occupational Stress

Since prevention is always better than cure, it would be the best part of stress management, if the occurrence of the circumstances or situations likely to cause stress are prevented to the possible extent at initial stage. Although some situations of stress are inevitable, part of occupational life or beyond control, effective interventions could be made at individual as well as organizational level to prevent the stressors or experience of stress.

At Individual Level

Since stress is a very subjective experience, it can be most effectively and conveniently prevented or dealt with through individual efforts. Most of the recent studies on stress management have proved the merits of individual-oriented techniques in preventing or reducing workers' distress (Murphy, 1984a). The individual-oriented interventions are more popular than organizational change approaches due to both logistic and conceptual factors. For example, individual-oriented programmes:

(1) are less or inexpensive and can be established and evaluated quickly without major disruption of work routines,
(2) focus on the workers, not the workplace as targets for change,
(3) address the issue of individual differences in perception of and reactions to stress, and
(4) can readily be incorporate into existing employee assistance and other company training programmes.

At individual level, stresses of job life can be prevented by making necessary restructuring and modifications in employees' cognitive and behaviour patterns, and by lowering their physiological arousals and stress reactions.

(i) *Cognitive Intervention Strategies*: Stress circumstances do not take their toll from a passive individual but from an individual who imbues stressful situations with personal meaning and struggles to control or master these situations. According to transactional model of stress (Lazarus, 1996; Lazarus & Folkman, 1984) experience of the reactions to stress largely depend upon focal person's cognitive appraisal of the stressful situation. In primary cognitive appraisal, an employee evaluates severity of the situation and the threats imposed by it. The severity of stress is determined by the employees' estimation of how much appears to be at stake in the transaction in term of their values, motives, or commitments. At the same time the focal person also evaluates (secondary appraisal) his capabilities and readily available resources to deal with the demands of the confronting situation. The final structure of the stress situation is based upon an equation that takes into account the amount and the probabilities of damage inherent in the threat as opposed to the individual's capacity to deal with it. The basic principle of cognitive model of stress reactions elaborates that "one's cognitive structure of a situation is an active and continuing process that includes successive appraisals of the external situation, and the risks, costs, and gains of a particular response. When the individual's vital interest appears to be at stake, the cognitive process provides a highly selective conceptualization. Depending upon the content of the cognitive constellation, the behavioural inclination may be a desire to flee, attack, approach or avoid." In conceptualizing a particular event, the cognitive set influences the picture obtained by an individual. Whether the mental image of the stress situation is broad, skewed, or narrow, clear or blurred, actual or distorted, depends upon the characteristics of the cognitive set. These cognitive sets determine which aspects are to be magnified, which to be minimized, and which to be excluded.

Kendall and Bennis (1983) suggested the following four guiding principles for cognitive-behaviour techniques:

1. Individuals do not respond directly to their environment, they respond to their own cognitive interpretation of the environment.
2. Cognitions (thoughts), emotions and behaviours (actions) are actually interrelated.
3. The prediction and understanding of negative cognitions and behaviours are enhanced by paying attention to a person's expectancies, beliefs, and attributions.
4. It is possible and desirable to integrate cognitive approaches to correcting problems with performance based and behavioural contingency management.

By developing some specific cognitive sets and patterns, and restructuring the situations, employees can prevent experiencing occupational stress to a considerable extent. Of course, for developing such stress-resistant cognitive patterns, the employee would require to make some specific modifications in their beliefs, attitudes, values, views, need-structure, attributions and orientations. The employee can manipulate the threatening qualities of stressors by desirably modified cognitive sets. The employee can cognitively prevent, moderate or tolerate the stresses of job life by:

1. Increasing objectivity in perception and evaluation of stressors and probable strains.

2. Avoiding misinterpretations, distortions, and exaggerations of a situation.
3. Increasing perspective—seeing the situations in a broader vista; obtaining a more relative concept of magnitude and seriousness of the situation of stress.
4. Intellectualization—analytical orientation towards threat of the whole situation.
5. Rationalization—providing plausible reason why situation should be upsetting.
6. Avoidant thinking—thinking about the things not relevant to the stressful aspects of the situation.
7. Cognitive avoidance of the situation.

Srivastava (1997) has prepared an inventory, in the form of rating scale, of stress-resistant cognitive-behavioural patterns which can be conveniently used as a tool in cognitive intervention programme. The employees may be trained to develop these cognitive patterns in order to prevent, moderate or cognitively cope with their occupational stress. The inventory consists of following stress-resistant cognitive patterns:

1. Consider difficult, adverse, or demanding job situations as inevitable part of job life.
2. Perceive stressful job situation as a temporary phase of the job.
3. Rationalize the situation of stress and its consequences.
4. Consider the demanding situation as an opportunity to learn, develop new skills, and to enhance self-confidence.
5. Take the excessive job demands as a challenge.
6. Assess the severity of your job stresses with reference to the others who are facing with similar or more severe stresses in their jobs.
7. Objectively think about why this situation of stress should have not arisen.
8. Believe that life is a mixture of sorrow and happiness.
9. Think that time itself takes care of such situations.

10. Accept the situations of stress thinking that there is nothing you can do to change them.
11. While dealing with the situation of stress, think about its positive outcomes.
12. Believe that every problem ultimately has some remedy.
13. Keep in mind that no one is totally free from stresses.
14. Accept the situations of stress as realities of life.
15. React to the hardships of job life with optimistic and positive affect.
16. Remind yourself that job is not everything.
17. Believe in Geeta's philosophy that "your right is to do your job only, not to the fruit thereof."
18. Accept the situations of stress as God's will.
19. Have faith in God and His kindness.

Ivancevich & Matteson (1987) have suggested "tolerance of stressors" at cognitive level as a primarily preventive technique. The employee can prevent or moderate the job stress by modifying their "cognitive appraisal" or by perspective taking "cognitive restructuring", and "cognitive rehearsing". The cognitive appraisal technique involves teaching employees to assess the severity of the stressor by considering the perspective in which they view a particular stress situation. More specially, employees are encouraged to ask themselves certain questions when a negative event is encountered. The focal employee should objectively analyze the actual causes of the occurrence of the situation of stress, and estimate its worst possible consequences. He must also think over the strategies to cope with stressful situation as well as the consequent outcomes. In addition, the employee might gain a new perspective by considering if any positive results might be associated with the negative event.

The "cognitive restructuring" technique of stress management is based on the premise that many people believe that other people or events are responsible for how they feel. The resulting beliefs can be irrational and quite often lead to increased stress. The aim of this intervention is to help employees cope with stress by changing their beliefs or cognitions. One model that has been proposed to understand this relationship is the A-B-C model where 'A' represents the activating event and 'C' denotes the consequences (feeling and behavioural) that occur in relation to the activating event. Cognitive restructuring concerns changing the 'B' component of the model, 'B' denotes the belief that occurs between the activating event and the consequences. For example, the rude behaviour of a customer, which might cause stress to the salesman, might be restricted by the belief that this behaviour was not against him but due to some of his or her (customer's) frustration. Matteson and Ivancevich (1987) noted the importance of keeping in mind that the objective of the cognitive restructuring is not to magically make people feel good about unpleasant events. Rather, the goal is to tolerate stressors by replacing negative feelings with neutral ones, or at least less negative ones.

Cognitive appraisal and cognitive restructuring are designed to help people tolerate stressors after they occur. A related technique, "cognitive rehearsal", involves helping employees tolerate stressors by anticipating them before they occur. This technique calls for visualizing a potentially stressful event before it occurs and practising or rehearsing how to respond to the imagined situation. This rehearsal should occur while the employee is relaxed and might include appraisal or restructuring as outlined above. By rehearsing to respond, the employee gets mentally prepared to face and deal with the situations of stress which might occur in future.

(ii) *Behavioural Intervention Strategies*: Since individual's thoughts, feeling and actions are interrelated, the individual who has developed stress-resistant cognitive patterns would also adopt certain behaviour patterns which help him preventing or coping with the situations of stress. By making some specific modifications in their habits, behavioural patterns and acquiring coping skills, the employees can prevent or moderate the stresses of their job life to a considerable extent. For example, the employees with Type A orientation can prevent or moderate their occupational stress by modifying their behaviour patterns, and by developing some behaviour patterns of Type B orientation. Though modification of certain existing dominant behaviour patterns are quite a difficult task, the employee can do so, to a considerable extent, through self-imposed behaviour modification method. The stress management practitioner can train the employees to learn the stress-resistant behaviour patterns and coping skills.

Following is an inventory of some stress-resistant behavioural patterns suggested by the author (1997):

1. Increase self-esteem and the level of tolerance and patience.
2. Do not be rigid in your ways of functioning, attitudes and decisions.
3. Recognize the potential sources of stress in your job.
4. Do things at work in a planned and systematic manner.
5. Try to separate, and maintain coordination among your job and other roles.
6. Avoid doing many things simultaneously.
7. Set your priorities for job activities.
8. Do work efficiently but avoid competitions.
9. Work on changing or modifying the style, methodology and policies which caused the situation or experience of stress.
10. Devote more time and energy to your job.
11. Discuss the problems with supervisor or/and other competent colleagues or superiors.
12. Try to maintain good relationship with your superiors, colleagues and subordinates, and have a few dependable friends.
13. Throw yourself into your job and work harder and sincerely.
14. Avoid time pressures and role overloading being regular and making proper distribution of the time for your job activities.
15. Avoid taking responsibilities or committing beyond your capability and resources.
16. Do not try to reach the perfection level in all routine job activities.

17. Be sincere, but do not be over enthusiastic all the time in discharging your duties.
18. Frankly tell your limitations and inabilities.
19. Try to find out complete or durable solutions to the job related problems.
20. Try to nip the problems in the bud.
21. Be a realist, aspire within the framework of your capabilities and resources.
22. Do not poke your nose in others or irrelevant affairs.
23. Try to overlook rather than to react to the irritating situations or behaviour of people at work.
24. Before doing something, consider all its possible consequences.
25. If there is no way out, do your best to get out of the situation gracefully.

Bhandarker and Singh (1986) evolved action plan for preventing or reducing managerial stress at individual, organizational, and social levels. At individual level, stress can be prevented or moderated by:

(1) cultivating belief in self,
(2) developing inner directed personality,
(3) developing self-coping mechanism by adopting the strategy of owning up to stress,
(4) relying on genuine problem solving strategies, and
(5) cultivating positive habits based on interests, such as yoga, meditation, sports and breathing exercise.

Singer (1960) long back suggested the following steps to avoid job tension at individual level:

(1) recognize the requirements of your job role,
(2) maintain perspective,
(3) keep a balance between work and recreation, and
(4) identify and accept your emotional needs.

Innovation Intervention Program: In the framework of behavioural (action) intervention for prevention of occupational stress, Bunce and West (1996) evolved "Innovation Intervention Program" for prevention of or coping with the stresses of job life. This program involves alternatively dealing with the problems which might cause strain. Herein employees at their own level innovate the strategies to change environmental pressures, barrier or procedures to prevent or reduce the stress at work. These innovations not only make the work environment less stressful, but also lead to the introduction of procedures which enhance productivity and quality of work. In their study, Bunce and West examined the effectiveness of Innovation Promotion Program IPP. The IPP opened with an overview of the subjects, with particular attention to the causes and manifestations of occupational strain. The program went on to introduce the concept of innovative coping. Participants having identified work-related stresses, were encouraged to develop innovative responses to those stressors through group discussion and individual action planning. The subjects were made aware of the factors which might help or hinder innovation. These factors included individual, group and organizational factors, as well as those intrinsic to the job and associated with working relations, which might influence the initiation and introduction of innovation. The study revealed that interventions promoting innovative responses reduced work related stress and improved innovation among the subjects.

Changing Stress-Inducing Behaviour Patterns: This is basically a stress-preventive strategy and also helps in combating the existent stressful situations. It has been empirically established that some specific personality and behaviour patterns increase individual's susceptibility to experience more stress and consequent strains. Mathney et al (1986) have suggested that by making necessary alteration in behavioural patterns, employees can prevent stress to a considerable extent. One useful construct in understanding this strategy is the Type A Behaviour Pattern (Friedman & Rosenman, 1974). The individuals diagnosed as being Type A are comparatively more competitive, hard driving, intense, have high need for control, have sense of time urgency, impatient, aggressive and hostile. These individuals are at a high risk for negative stress reactions. Treatment of the individuals exhibiting these behavioural pattern has been the subject of a great deal of research, but specific findings which lead to treatment have not been conclusive. It is not very clear as to which aspects of their behavioural, psychological, or emotional functioning make them vulnerable to physical strains. Thus, there is no clear direction for an intervention. I personally feel that it is quite difficult to markedly change or modify the behavioural patterns at an advanced stage of life. Behavioural patterns become the part of one's personality as it is structured as a result of contribution of the factors like heredity, personality traits, motivational structure, and socio-cultural environment. It can be changed or modified at an early stage of an individual's development. However, efforts have been made to implement stress management for Type A individuals. Suinn (1982) has developed a behaviour modification programme for heart patients, which included the training in muscle relaxation, identifying varying degrees of muscle tension, general relaxation, and using imagery to practise behaviour incompatible with Type A behaviour. Powell (1984) also suggested some programmes such as playing to lose in sports, preparing a log of things which lead to anger, and laughing at oneself. An extensive treatment programme has been extended by Roskies (1987) in her book *Stress Management for the Healthy Type A*. The programme has been divided into eight modules as shown in Table 4.1.

Table 4.1
Stress Management Programmes For Type A Individuals

Modules	*Skills to be Taught*
Introduction to the programme	General overview
Relax: learning to control physical stress responses.	Self monitoring of physical and emotional tension signs; progressive muscle relaxation.
Control yourself: learning to control behavioural stress responses.	Self monitoring of behavioural signs of tension; incompatible behaviours, delay,communication skills.
Think productively: learning to control cognitive stress responses.	Self monitoring of self-talk; cognitive restructuring.
Be prepared: learning to anticipate and plan for predictable stress situations.	Identification of recurrent stress triggers; stress inoculation training.
Cool it: learning emergency braking in unpredictable stress situations.	Identification of signs of heightened tension; application of physical, behavioural and cognitive controls; anger control.
Building stress resistance: learning to plan for rest and recuperation.	Identification of pleasurable activities; problem solving.
Protecting your investment: stress management as a lifelong investment.	Relapse prevention.

Stress Inoculation Training: This technique of stress management, developed by Meichenbaum (1977), combines the cognitive and behavioural strategies. Stress inoculation training focuses on altering the way an individual processes information about a stressful situation and identifies ways of reacting to it (Ivancevich & Matteson, 1988). This approach has been used to help people with a variety of stress reactions including anger, anxiety and fear. The training includes following three stages (Table 4.2).

Table 4.2

Stages of Stress Inoculation Training

Stage	*Description*
1. Preparation	Educating the employee about the relationship between maladaptive thoughts and behaviour patterns, and convincing him that he can cope with the situations of stress.
2. Skill training	Helping the employee confront stressful situations by using coping skills he already has or by developing new coping skills.
3.Application training	Getting the employee to practise and apply newly developed skills.

These techniques improve the means by which an individual can tolerate stressors by focusing on the relationship between thoughts and actions. These techniques serve as powerful tools in assisting employees to recognize that they can help controlling stress conditions by changing their thinking.

Developing Coping Skills and Resources: The first intervention among combative strategies to be taken up at an individual level, focuses on developing coping resources. In fact, the preventive interventions help in developing coping resources to some extent. Assertiveness is a preventive strategy, but it becomes a combative strategy when it is used to deal with already existing problem. Acquisition of social skill is another source of coping. Research findings suggest that social support is effective in combating stress (Wells, 1984).

Social support reduces employees' stress in three ways:

(i) social support can directly enhance health by satisfying social needs for affiliation, approval, appreciation, and security;
(ii) social support can reduce inter-person tension at work and directly affects the level of stress;
(iii) social support also buffers the relationship of occupational stress and consequent strains.

Time management has been found to be another useful method for helping workers in developing coping responses. The employee can prevent as well as combat with the stresses of role overload and conflicts through effective management of his time and prioritization of job activities or duties. The time management strategies are often focused on two areas: knowledge or information acquisition and skill development. For effective time management the employee should have adequate knowledge of job responsibilities, duties and authorities. One way to intervene is to have employees work with supervisors to clarify expectations associated with specific jobs and identify the task and whether the employee has to act alone or enlist the support of others. The employee must be trained how to allocate time among his different duties at work. By maintaining the log of the time spent on different duties the employee can allocate/reallocate the time in proper and convenient manner.

Besides the management of time, the employee should also determine the priorities for his different job activities. It is often seen that in absence of schedules and priorities majority of the workers spent more than fifty per cent of their time in non-productive activities. Completing the given task in time has no meaning sometimes if their priority has not been taken into consideration. Effective time management training should include instructions and exercises that encourage workers to schedule and prioritize duties of their jobs. Besides the priorities at work, employees should also determine the priorities among their roles on-and off-the-job. The employees should also take into consideration their career goals and values in determining the priorities. Finally, time management interventions should also help them in identifying 'time robbers', such as meetings, visitors, paperwork, trouble shooting, phone calls, etc. The employees should be trained to conserve time, to control time, and to make time by adopting convenient methods and behavioural changes.

Monitoring Stressors and Stress Symptoms: One of the primarily preventive strategies, as suggested by Mathney et al (1994), is focusing on the symptoms of job stress. The employees can avoid stress, to a possible extent, if they become aware of potential stressors of job life and the symptoms which lead to stress reaction. One technique under this category of strategy is to maintaining a stress diary which is a personal record of the events that happen before a negative stress response (Ivancevich & Matteson, 1980). The employee would enter in the log a specific description of the events along with a description of the feelings and thoughts that resulted from the event. The individual would also note the time of day when he noticed these symptoms or feelings. Along with the symptoms the focal employee would also enter in the diary the events which have caused these symptoms of stress. The employee must be advised to keep the log for an extended period of time. The practitioner should help the individual in analyzing the results of the stress diary. The analysis should identify the themes or patterns that point to specific kind of stress responses in relation to specific events, so that specific intervention could be planned in the light of pattern of relationship between stressors and specific responses to them. On the basis of the case of an employee specific interventions have been suggested by the counsellor for certain stress situations and symptoms in the Table 4.3 (Ref. Ross & Altmaier, 1994).

Table 4.3
Preventive Interventions for Stress Situation/Symptoms

Stress Situations/ Symptoms	*Interventions*
Muscle tension	Review progressive muscle relaxation exercises with employees.
Stress reactions preceded by meeting with boss.	Examine the relationship between employees and the boss and develop strategy to improve it.
Consistent pattern of not completing work that was planned for a given day.	Discuss time-management skills. See whether daily goals being set are realistic.

Developing Personal Resources: Another preventive strategy, suggested by Mathney et al., (1986), involves the development of certain behavioural skills which prepare the employee to cope with stressful situations when they occur. The specific strategies which are included in this category are training in social skills and problem solving skills that help employees cope with social interactions which might lead to stress. By developing their skills the individual prevents the occurrence of stressful situations. Researchers have developed interventions for social skills training for enabling the employees to prevent the experience of stress arising from "social anxiety". These skills help an individual in interacting more conveniently with each others. Jaremko (1983) developed a programme for socially anxious individuals which includes training, initiating and maintaining conversations, making and refusing requests, making and receiving criticisms, giving and receiving complements, and interpreting non-verbal cues in the behaviour of others.

"Assertiveness training" is another important component of social skill training. The training helps the individuals in responding in a straightforward manner with regard to what they believe, feel, and wish. Another important subset of social skills to prevent the social stresses is "problem solving skills" (Mathney, et al., 1986). These skills help the individual to respond with some action that will reduce the stressfulness of a situation. The employees may be trained to develop the skills which would help them to be more creative or pro-active in reaching solutions to stressful situations. Effective communication and negotiation skills also help the employee in dealing with certain stressful social or interpersonal situations.

***Making Adjustments Between Work-Family Roles*:** Among the combating stress management strategies, particularly for single parents and dual career couples, is to make adjustments between job and family lives. It is a practical and easy intervention. Interventions should be made to help the employees to make good adjustment between the demands of job, marital and family roles. Organizations are only beginning to respond to the needs of the changing workplace: It is role of human service practitioners to help individuals cope with the stresses they encounter when their work and family lives conflict.

One possible intervention strategy is to offer guidance and training to individuals who attempt to balance the demands of work and home life. Effective communication skills will be helpful for dual-career couples who cope with two partners' careers. Similarly, negotiation and assertiveness training would prove beneficial for the parents who try to propose an alternative work schedule to accommodate child care needs. Time management skills might help a single parent in coping with the demands of work and home. Interviewing several hundred people, Dynerman and Hayes (1991) have compiled a series of practical suggestions for planning work-home interface stressors, negotiating flexible work options, and dealing with jobs after a creative work schedule or situation has been developed.

(iii) *Physiological Intervention Strategies*: Physiological strategies for prevention of stress have also been noted as effective interventions, and their popularity is consistently increasing all over the world. It is an established fact that human body prepares itself to respond to stresses by changing certain bodily functions such as heart rate, blood flow, muscle tensions, etc. These physiological changes can lead to the symptoms of stress if they are prolonged. Stress management practitioners have suggested a set of interventions which help individuals in preventing the negative effects of stress by lowering physiological arousal, such as deep breathing, progressive muscle relaxation, physical exercises, biofeedback, autogenic training, yoga and meditation.

***Deep Breathing*:** A very simple but useful technique for lowering down the physiological arousal is deep breathing. The individual must be advised to breathe more deeply from the abdomen, instead of shallow (thoracic) breaths which are associated with stress response. Physiological arousal is affected by this technique because of the close association between breathing centre and reticular activating system (RAS) in the brain. Matteson and Ivancevich (1987) reported that the RAS controls neuro-muscular functioning and, thus, deep breathing leads to relaxation in the neuro-muscular system. Mason (1980) noted positive results of the intervention of deep breathing.

***Progressive Muscle Relaxation*:** It is an extension to the technique of deep breathing, developed long back by Jacobson (1938). In the technique of progressive muscle relaxation the individual assumes a comfortable position and begins to breathe deeply. Then, the individual relaxes groups of muscles one at a time, beginning with the feet muscles. Jacobson argues that through this technique the mind gets relaxed because the relaxed muscles are associated with a decrease in emotional tension. He recommended to practice this exercise twice a day for 15 to 20 minutes.

***Aerobic Exercise*:** Physical exercise is another effective and popular means of preventing stress-effects by lowering arousal in recent years. Besides the health benefits, physical exercise has been found to result in psychological well being. Stress is said to be triggered by a 'fight or flight' response (the alarm stage of the General Adaptation Syndrome) which includes changes in heart rate, blood pressure, hormonal secretion, and muscle tension. Matteson and Ivancevich (1987) explains that the purpose of the fight or flight response is to prepare the body for action. In many stressful situations action does not follow exposure to the stressor. Thus, exercise can act as a release for these physical processes. Research has shown that routine vigorous activity is an effective strategy for preventing the negative effects of stress. Regarding the preventive effect of exercise on stress response, Jette (1984) has concluded that three variables are important, i.e., type, frequency and duration of exercise. The type of exercise that produces the most effects is aerobic exercise (i.e. jogging, cycling, walking, and swimming). Aerobic exercise refers to repetitive movement of large muscle groups in which energy is derived from aerobic metabolism. In terms of frequency, these exercises should be done normally three to four times a week. The duration of these exercise sessions should be about 30 to 40 minutes at 50 to 60 per cent of maximal working capacity. Compliance is an important factor in physical exercises and its effects. Strategies such as goal setting and use of distraction or dissociation during exercise may improve compliance. Martin and Dubbert (1987) have suggested that exercise programme should: (1) be convenient, (2) use group exercise formats, (3) use a participant/supervisor, (4) emphasize individual responsibility for exercise, (5) enforce the exercise habit, (6) use generalization training, and (7) use continued feedback and testings.

With regard to psychological effects of exercise, investigations have reported that both acute exercise and chronic exercise lead to improvement in mood, such as decreased anxiety and depression and increased feeling of vigour (Boutcher & Landers, 1989; Roth & Holmes, 1987). These exercises have been reported to prevent or resist the experience of stress. The primary rationale for examining the effects of exercise and stress responses stemmed from the fact that improved physical fitness reduces autonomically mediated cardiovascular responses to physical stress; therefore it is assumed that responses to psychological stress might likewise be reduced. Findings of some studies confirmed the assumption revealing that physical exercise training reduces plasma norepinephrine concentration (Meredith et al., 1990). Thus, there is indirect support to the hypothesis that exercise reduces responses to stress by altering automatic sensitivity.

Research both in human and animal subjects suggest that acute exercise reduces stress and certain physical response to stress such as blood pressure and cardiovascular reactivity. Pironnet and associates (1989) found decreased adrenergic responses to physiological and mental tasks following two hours of cycle ergometry. In addition to its effect on physicological responses to stress, exercise has also been found to affect subjective mood states. Results of the investigations suggest that both acute and chronic exercise may reduce anxiety and depression. In an other study, psychological tension was significantly reduced by moderate or intense exercises. Swimming has also been noted to reduce anger, tension, depression and confusion, and an increase in vigour (Berger & Owen, 1983).

Biofeedback (Electromyographic): In general, biofeedback system operates by detecting changes in the biological environment of the affected person by means of visual and auditory signals. The individual using these precise and immediate information, engages in a trial and error strategy of testing in order to make change in signals in the desired direction. By biofeedback as a guide, the individual learns in relatively short order how to control the biological response system generating the biofeedback signals. Biofeedback essentially involves three stages. The first stage is acquiring awareness of the maladaptive response. By means of biofeedback the client learns that certain thoughts as well as bodily events influence the response in question. Next, guided by the biofeedback signal, the individual learns to control the response. Finally the client learns to transfer the control into day-to-day life.

Biofeedback as a technique of stress management developed out of the work in the field of psychology and physiology. In psychology work with laboratory animals in operant conditioning studies led to the discovery that animals could be trained to control certain autonomic bodily functions. This observation was extended to human beings, where it was found that receiving immediate feedback or information on physiological factors could lead to individuals learning to control visceral parameters including brain waves, heart rate, muscle tension, body temperature, stomach acidity and blood pressure. Using this methodology biofeedback has been involved in treating disease and in reducing physiological responses associated with stress. Special equipment is used to alert the individual to physiological changes. To monitor these changes sensors are attached to the body. The most common of these sensors are electrical sensors used to detect myocardial activity, muscle tension and brainwave activity. Similarly, transducers are used to measure blood pressure and photoplelhysmographs are used to measure pulse pressure (Matteson & Ivancevich, 1987). Two types of biofeedback have been developed: operant conditioning and augmented feedback. Operant conditioning biofeedback involves using physiological information as a reinforce to bring about the desirable physiological changes. Augmented biofeedback is more commonly used as a technique for stress management which involves providing the individual with continuous feedback about physiological functioning (Brown, 1984).

Biofeedback has been found to be effective in helping individuals in restoring their bodies to non-stressed states. In their study Matteson and Ivancevich (1987) found that biofeedback training reduced chronic tension, headache and significantly decreased the interference of stress-related symptoms. However, other studies have not found significant positive results of biofeedback training. It is a time-consuming and costly method. Better results could be obtained spending the money and effort on other conventional stress management interventions.

Autogenic Training and Stress Management: The German neurologist Schultz is credited with the development of "Autogenic Training" (AT), which he described as a self-hypnotic procedure. The term "autogenic", derived from the Greek words *autos* and *genos*, can aptly be translated as "self-exercised or self-induction therapy". The rejected psychoanalysis is promising treatment for psychosomatic disturbances. He was of the opinion that "it is complete non-sense to shoot with psychoanalytic guns after symptom sparrows". The development of AT as a novel technique appears to be based on two sources: Schultz's own experiences with clinical hypnosis, and Vogt's observations in brain research. However, it may not be equated with hypnosis, nor it is simply another form of relaxation therapy. This method has been described as a "psychop- hysiological self-control therapy", or "psychophysiologic form of psychotherapy which the patient carries out himself by using passive concentration upon certain combinations of psychophysiologically adapted stimuli". AT' is unique as an autonomic self-regulation therapy with emphasis on "self-control". Schultz believed that the self-regularly capacities and ultimately the self-healing powers of body may be left alone to do its work. Homeostatic model and biological self-regulation theory (Linden, 1988) were foreshadowed by Schultz when he conceptualized AT. The objective of AT is to permit self-regulation in either direction (i.e. deep relaxation or augmentation of a physiological activity) through "passive concentration" or "self-hypnosis". In this method, the trainee concentrates on his sensations in a passive manner, without trying to bring about change. The trainee is instructed to concentrate on inner sensations rather than environmental stimuli. Here, the trainee is instructed not to force for concentration but to allow sensations to happen. He must be simply an observer rather than a manipulator.

Autogenic Biofeedback Training: Elmer Green and Alyce who confounded and developed the autogenic biofeedback treatment methods decided to pursue their interest in the development of human awareness and volition in order to develop ways of teaching people to become conscious of and to learn control of normally unconscious physiological and psychological processes. Autogenic training, a system of psychosomatic self-regulation, permits the gradual acquisition of autonomic control. The biofeedback training refers to a collection of techniques useful in accelerating psychosomatic self-regulation. Autogenic biofeedback training integrates these two self-regulatory techniques. It provides a methodology combining the best features of each. This integrative method has wide range applications in medicine psychology, and education. Green developed a plan to study control of conscious processes through their physiological correlates in autonomic nervous function. Autogenic biofeedback training has begun to emerge on a variety of topics, including deep relaxation, voluntary control of internal psychological and physiological states, self-regulation and healing, creativity, migraine, headaches and anxiety and tension reduction.

Yoga and Meditation: Yoga and transcendental meditation are the systems of Indian philosophy and practice. These techniques have been in use in India since ancient times as the techniques of relief from stress and for improvement in physical and psychological health. In contemporary societies importance and need of yoga has been realized by the people all over the world. It is being used as preventive as well as therapeutic technique. Yoga has now become a popular technique for stress management. The word "Yoga" means union of human being and universal energy. It teaches the means by which one can learn to communicate with the "Absolute" or with universal energy (Patel, 1993). A human being consists of both material and non-material entities. The material entity is physical body with all its organs and the non-material entities are soul and mind. Yoga attempts to bring within its perspective all three sides of human life, i.e., body, mind and soul. The physical dimension of human life also includes the natural elements such as air, water, food and sunshine without which humans cannot sustain physical life, and a healthy body is necessary to house the inner soul. Yoga, by presenting us with various values, techniques and disciplines, teaches us ways of establishing harmony among various sides of life (Patel, 1993). Different types of yoga have been developed by Indian Yogis, such as "Hatha Yoga"— the physical path for the development of the body; "Gyan Yoga"— the intellectual path; "Bhakti Yoga"— devotional path; "Karma Yoga"— the path of practical actions for the unfolding of the mind and realization of the soul. The different paths for developing the mind are based on the fact that the mind has three different aspects, i.e., knowing, feeling, and willing. In some people intellect predominates, in others emotion, and in still others action. For intellectuals, the yoga of knowledge (Gyan) is prescribed; for emotional people, the devotional (Bhakti) yoga of love and faith; and for the people of action, the yoga based on daily action (Karma) is prescribed. However, this does not mean that intellect, emotion and action are exclusive of one another. Although one quality dominates in each individual, and the individual can thus benefit from adopting the suitable path, it is important to allow cross-currents from other systems to intermingle. In "Raja Yoga" all the systems converge.

Hatha Yoga: The main components of Hatha Yoga are: (1) regulation of mind and the body through different breathing exercises; (2) over 200 balanced physical postures to exercise every muscle in the body in order to prevent skelete muscular deterioration, to tone up all organs in the body and insure their healthy functioning; (3) exercise for awakening "kundalini" (reservoir of energy believed to be situated at the base of the spinal cord) and making this energy toward higher power.

Gyan Yoga: This path leads to knowledge of one's self. "Who am I"? is the problem the person of knowledge must solve. According to yoga philosophy ignorance is the cause of pain and misery in life. The lack of discrimination between temporary and permanent, real and unreal, truth and untruth, and self and non-self is at the roots of illness and diseases. Intellectual exercise involves learning to discriminate between each of these through the process of self-analysis. It is something like cognitive approach in psychological terminology.

The first step in gyan yoga is asking "Am I my body"? Here one should realize that "I" does mean "my physical body" because "I" exists when even some organs of my body or sensations are lost. So the "self " or "I" is not the body, but it is the centre of consciousness. Second step involves asking "Am I my mind?" Am I what my mind thinks or feels, desires, hates, anger, likes, dislikes, fears, greeds, sympathises, hostiles or other thoughts or feelings? According to Gyan Yoga, I does mean mind or feelings and emotions because some people (yogis) withdraw from all experiences of the outer would and from all emotions, but the sense of self-existence still remains there. It is possible to disassociate one's self from the body and the mind through yoga. The faint recognition of dispassionate pure consciousness is the essence of self-knowledge. When the knowledge of self is realized, following six attainments are thought to be achieved (Siddhantalankar & Taraporevala, 1969):

(1) The agitation and passion of the mind subside, and the mind finds rest in peace and harmony.

(2) With knowledge of the spiritual entity separate from the physical body, it becomes possible to control body-pain and pleasure, heat and cold, etc.

(3) There is willing acceptance of one's worldly possessions as well as of the persons one is associated with in life. One should accept willingly whatever one gets after making the necessary efforts.

(4) One attains endurance of the hardship of life with a smiling face.

(5) One develops an abiding faith and confidence in the design of the grand plan of the universe by the Supreme Power.

(6) Steadfastness, firmness of purpose, constancy, and resolution comprise a settled condition of the mind.

***Bhakti Yoga*:** The essence of the Bhakti yoga or devotional path is love and sacrifice (Siddhantalankar & Taraporevala, 1969). It is an emotion of heart. The relationship between the devotee and the object of devotion between the soul and the personal God is like the relationship between love and beloved. The devotional path involves concentration on the object of devotion with constancy and faith. "Concentration" means that one is required to enter the cord of the object of devotion and love until one feels totally merged into it and feels one with it. One completely loses the sense of his separate identity. This theme has been described in *Bhagavad Gita* as "*Mayyev Mana Aaditswa, Mayi Buddhi Niveshaya*", which means "Fix your mind on Me and establish your intellect in Me alone" (*Bhagavad Gita*-XII: 8). "Constancy" here means always, day and night and every single moment. The third element of devotion is "faith". It is not blind faith, but the faith that comes from factual and truthful experience. The devotee surrenders consciousness to the "Super Consciousness", all thoughts, feelings, and actions are surrendered to God.

Karma Yoga : The law of "karma" is the spiritual counterpart of the physical law of the cause and effect. According to this principle, human beings are inextricably bound up in the wheel of cause and effect by their past and present actions. The time span covers not only this life but also past and future lives. Persons who are suffering through what they see as no fault of their own are likely to believe that it is injustice, and may rebel against God. But according to law of karma there is no point accusing God or fate for the apparent injustice. Goods and evils acquired through deeds by the soul throughout many incarnations are manifested as enduring characteristics from one incarnation to another, being modified by further karmas. According to the philosophy of karma, what we are in the present life is determined by what we have acted in previous lives, and what we do in present life will decide our future in this life as well as in lives to come. As the human soul passes through from one life to another, it learns new lessons, gathers new experiences, and learns to recognize the pain that comes from wrong actions and happiness that comes from right and good actions. We are not awarded for our good deeds, but we receive our rewards through and by characteristics and qualities we acquire. People often do not believe that they remember the experience of past lives. But karma yoga philosophy insists that these experiences, though not remembered, are not lost to us. They become part of the material of which our minds are composed, and are indelibly imprinted on the fabric of our characters. They exist in the form of our feelings, characteristics, inclinations, likes, dislikes, affinities and repulsions. According to Karma Yoga philosophy, we should strive to make our actions good, honest and desirable without expecting fruits thereof. It is expectations which bring sorrow or give frustration if not fulfilled. Attachment is the cause of every suffering and frustrations. The only way to get rid of sorrow is non-attachment.

It seems that the acceptance of the law of karma can

dissolve age, hurt, jealousy, mistrust or resentment, and can strengthen our resolve to improve and became wiser. The law of karma teaches us to share and care, be compassionate and kind, and reach out to others for the ultimate good of our souls and destinies. By practising Karma Yoga, employees can largely prevent, moderate or cope with their stresses at cognitive as well as behaviour level.

***Raja Yoga*:** Raja yoga is an integration of all systems of yoga and denoted as a kind of yoga. The exponent of this yoga was Patanjali. He extended teachings to fight against the afflictions of humankind over 2000 years ago. It has an "eightfold spiritual path" involving eight steps, namely:

(1) "Yama", or the five abstentions (i.e. abstentions from violence, lying, stealing, sexuality, and greed);
(2) "Niyama", or five observances (i.e. purification, contentment, self-discipline, studiousness, and surrender to God;
(3) "Aasanas", or balanced exercise postures;
(4) "Pranayam", or regulation of breath;
(5) "Pratyahara", or withdrawal of senses;
(6) "Dharana", of concentration;
(7) "Dhyana", or contemplation;
(8) "Samadhi", or the meditative state.

The most important ingredient in the practice of this yoga is faith. The physical postures in this yoga involve learning to control, regulate, and become aware of one's physical existence. During the various exercises, breathing bears a certain relationship to the sequence of the body movements. One is required to give complete mental attention to each movement, to the exclusion of everything else. Through practice, this awareness is heightened to such an extent that it falls in the field of consciousness. By regularly practising concentration on body movements, the practitioner gradually strengthens his own personality and different body functions become more integrated with one another as well as with personality. Regulation of breathing enables one to reach the innermost consciousness. The stage of the withdrawal of the senses involve deep muscle relaxation of the body. The reason for observing this rule is to cut down on visceral impulses going to the brain. The next three stages—concentration, contemplation, and meditative state—together form the practice of meditation.

Meditation: Meditation has been part of most of Eastern and Western cultures and religions. It is probably the oldest method of yoga. Recently medical people have realized that it can be used without any religious connotation in the promotion of health. Meditation involves taking a comfortable position—either sitting, lying down, or standing. But sitting is the most useful and common posture. It then involves being in a quiet environment, regulating the breath, adopting a physically relaxed and mentally positive attitude and dwelling single mindedly upon an object. The object of the concentration in meditation does not have to be physical. It can be an idea or image; it can be mental repetition of a word or phrase (mantra); it can be observing one's own thoughts, perception, or reaction; or it can be concentrating on some bodily generated rhythm. In religious practice, the object of concentration is God. As the deeper state of concentration is developed, the process becomes more intimate and compelling. The mind that holds an idea becomes held by it. Again, this power of subconscious can be used to build character. It is actually a state of the greatest silence, an experience of bliss. An other way to describe, meditation is—an experience, a state of being.

The practical advantages of meditation are that we can function more efficiently, feel more complete in ourselves and realize more of our potentials. We feel closer to ourselves and are better able to relate to others. Our personality structure is strengthened and becomes more integrated. We are able to think and express ourselves with more clarity. We are more effective in our work and clear in our goals. Other physiological advantages include induction of oxygen consumption, respiratory rate, and cardiac output (indicating metabolic rest); a marked decrease in blood lactake level (reduction in anxiety); increase in electrical resistance of the skin (indicating autonomic rest); and increase in alpha brainwaves (indicating mental rest) (Wallace & Benson, 1972).

Meditation in Action: In this approach, at frequent intervals during the day, if we observe our mind to see what it is doing, it becomes clear that mind is busy with wishful thinking, daydreaming, and fantasies of the future. Such useless activities waste time and energy, and lowers the quality of our work. By learning to concentrate on everyday tasks as if it that was the most important thing at that moment, and by understanding that each task is a part of the total harmony with the universe, we become closer to reality. When a person is completely engrossed in whatever he or she is doing he is meditating in the action.

Practical Instructions for Meditation

Patel (1993) has suggested following instructions for the practice of meditation:

1. Meditate where the distraction of noise, movement, light, and activity of other people are within tolerance level.
2. Ensure your physical and mental comfort. Do not practice at least for two hours after a meal. It is beneficial to practice twice a day, for about 15 to 20 minutes each time.
3. Adopt a poised posture. The eyes should be closed and the body should be relaxed.
4. Breath through the nostrils and down into abdomen. Breathing should be regular, slow, and rhytharial.
5. Dwell single mindedly on an object of meditation. This can be a physical object, a word or phrase repeated mentally or aloud.
6. Passive awareness is very important. You must develop a passive and relaxed attitude toward distraction. You will find that thoughts and images will flit in and out of your mind. Each time you become conscious that your mind has wandered away, just bring it back to the object of your meditation. Do this as many times as is necessary, always maintain relaxed and passive attitude. As

you become more experienced, distracting thoughts and images will lessen. Accept that they are inevitable and maintain an attitude of indifference to them. Meditation is received if you keep thinking about meditation.

7. Practice regularly. With practice it become easier to still the mind.

Among the modern forms of meditation, "transcendental meditation" (TM) is most widely known and studied. It may be more accurately described as "transitional" because it retains certain cultic features such as "puja". Among the clinically oriented meditation techniques, "Clinically standardized meditation" (Carrington, 1978) and the "Respiratory one method" (Benson, 1975) have been the most widely used to date. These techniques were devised with clinical objectives in mind and are strictly non-cultic. The "clinically standardized meditation" is relatively permissive technique and may be subjectively experienced as almost effortless. In this method, the trainee selects a sound from a standard list of sounds and then repeats this sound mentally, without internally linking the sound to the breathing pattern or pacing it in any structured manner. In "respiratory one method" the trainee repeats the word "one" to himself mentally, and at the same time intentionally linking this word with each exhalation. Thus, it is a relatively disciplined form of meditation with two objects—the chosen word and the breath. Buddhist "mindfulness" meditation is also a common non-concentrative method. But it is a less standardized method being used in clinical settings. It is more difficult method to learn. Success of the trainee depends more on the individual expertise and personality of the trainer.

Relaxation: The state associated with transcendental meditation (TM) is achieved when physical and mental relaxations are at a peak. A meditation technique developed by Benson (1975) is similar to TM. In this technique the individual assumes a comfortable position and begins deep breathing. The individual focuses passive attention on a single word, although not a sacred word as is the 'mantra' in TM. Benson proposed that using this technique summons forth a state labelled the "relaxation-response", said to be the opposite to the body's response to stress. This technique can be taught by a TM instructor (Matteson & Ivancevich, 1987) as given in Table 4.4.

Relaxation is a form of meditation—a state of concentration. By using the mind to focus upon an object, image, or thought, one cancels out all distraction associated with everyday life, and counter balances the stress response.

Relaxation response has four elements:

1. A quiet environment—to turn off external distractions.
2. A comfortable position—sitting or kneeling with back straight, no tight clothing.
3. As object thought, or image to dwell upon (repetition of a word or sound such as 'one', focusing upon breathing, or saying, "I am relaxed").
4. A passive attitude—allowing an emptying of distracting thoughts.

With regular practice once or twice a day for 10-15 minutes, the following results are possible :

During relaxation you will experience:

1. A decrease in the rate of metabolism, a restful state with a drop in heart rate and respiratory rate.
2. A marked decrease in the body's oxygen consumption.
3. A decrease in blood pressure.
4. A decrease in muscle tension.

After relaxation, you may notice carry over effects including:

1. Lower response to stress-less anxiety.
2. Better coping abilities.
3. A new found acceptance of self, more tolerant of own weaknesses or limitations.
4. Improved learning ability, better retention and recall.
5. A sense of calm, of being collected—a more quiet, philosophical attitude.

The above-mentioned techniques, though difficult to learn, have been found to be quite effective in preventing, the psychosomatic problems (such as hypertension, blood pressure, coronary heart diseases, asthma, etc.), and coping with the stresses of day-to-day life by increasing resistance and lower down the arousal. However, these techniques have not been frequently used as intervention in the management of occupational stress. Thought it is difficult to adopt these methods, it can be of great help in preventing and coping with the stresses of job life and adapting to the consequent strains. The practice of these exercises by the employees can lower down their physiological arousals, and prepares their body to respond to stress by changing certain bodily functions such as heart rate, blood pressure, muscle tension, which can produce stress symptoms if they are prolonged.

Psychoeducational Preventive Program

By combining physiological, behavioural, and cognitive preventive interventions Kagan, Kagan and Watson (1994) developed the psychoeducational preventive model for prevention or reduction of job stress. This model, instead of reducing environmental stressors, encompasses the human functions. They proposed the following taxonomy of psychoeducational interventions for preventing or reducing stress, which includes from controlling one's physiological reactions, to skill to influence others, to self-awareness:

1. Physiological reactions: Experience of stress can be prevented or reduced by improving ability to control one's own physiological reactions to environmental events likely to cause stress. These physiological reactions include progressive muscle relaxation training, meditation, nutrition, etc.

2. Skill for coping with people: Stress reduction is also assumed to occur through increased confidence and skills to have an impact on and change other people rather than changing one self. The methods to cater these abilities and skills include assertiveness, training, microcounselling, human relations training, and preventive training to cope with stress caused by unexpected or threatening interpersonal events in the environment.

3. Self and interpersonal awareness: Stress can also be reduced through increased self-understanding and self-awareness of cognitive and affective reactions to interpersonal events. These skills may be developed through insight therapy, cognitive-affective therapy, stress management, and interpersonal process recall.

Kagan et al. (1994) examined the effectiveness of their intervention model in a sample of the employees of emergency medical services. The study established the effectiveness of the psychoeducational programme in reducing job stress and its consequences.

Stress Prevention at Organization Level

The situations which cause or are likely to cause stress to the employees can also be prevented by adopting certain precautionary and corrective interventions at organizational level. The executives of the organizations, who are concerned with their own stress as well as of other employees of different levels, must identify the probable sources or causes of stress and nip them in bud by taking necessary precautions and by adopting corrective interventions to the feasible extent at organizational level.

At initial organizational level, selection of suitable personnel and their proper training in the framework of the job requirements can largely help in preventing or mitigating the job stress likely to be caused by a misfit between employee and his job demands and from job difficulty. While selecting employees, their needs, values and attitudes should also be assessed, besides the assessment of their skills and aptitudes. This congruence between employee and his job can also be attained through "job characteristics" approach to task-design. The job design approach attempts at linking the individual to the job characteristics, with expected outcomes of high intrinsic motivation, high performance and job satisfaction and low absenteeism. The job factors and work environment which could create stress may also be prevented by the manager in collaboration with of technical experts. Proper job design and job enrichment can also prevent job stress or keep its level within desirable limits.

Proper training of new employees and orientation to already working employees also can prevent the experience of stress in work setting. Training has been identified as an important component of interventions to deal with occupational stress. Several areas of training should be pursued with regard to stress management: helping individual's cope, teaching managers about the importance of job design, and inform workers about the job factors that increase the risk of psychological disorders.

Managers should also identify the potential sources of stress in work environment and make efforts to remove, correct or control them to the maximum possible extent through effective corrective interventions. At this level, job roles can be clearly defined and allocated in order to prevent or minimize the stress likely to arise from role ambiguities and role conflicts. Stress of role overload can be dealt with by reducing role demands and job rotation.

Improvement in interpersonal relations at work afford the greatest difficulty. However, interpersonal compatibility should be a consideration in assignments and promotions of employees in order to avoid sociopsychological stress in work environment. Management may foresee the potential conflicts and pressures, and adopt necessary measures to avoid them. Supportive supervision and interpersonal relations at work also can prevent the occurrence of the situations of interpersonal stress.

Organizational role is a prominent and frequent cause of stress experienced by most of the employees. Various types of inadequacies, ambiguities, and conflicts in job role result in severe stress to its occupants. Pestonjee (1989) has suggested the specific functional strategies to avoid/prevent the occurrence of different types of role stress. These strategies are summarized in Table 4.5.

Table 4.4
Preventive Strategies for Role Stress

Role Stressors	*Preventive Strategies*
Self-role distance	Role integration
Inter-role distance	Role negotiation
Role stagnation	Role transition
Role isolation	Role linkage
Role ambiguity	Role clarification
Role expectation conflicts	Role making
Role overload	Role slimming
Role erosion	Role development/enrichment
Resource inadequacy	Resource generation
Personal inadequacy	Role linkage

***Socialization and Orientation of New Employees*:** When a new employee joins an organization, he is faced with the task of becoming adjusted to new work environment. This period of employees' socialization has great potential for stress. Matteson and Ivancevich (1987) noted three stages through which individuals must pass as they enter the organization: getting in, breaking in, and settling in. In the first stage, the employees face new environment and demands. In the stage of breaking in the individual learns about the organization including relationship with co-workers, new job tasks, role clarification, bureaucratic procedures, etc. Finally, in settling in phase of socialization, employee comes to resolve two types of conflicts: the conflicting demands of work and others in the environment and the conflicting demands of on-the-job and off-the-job lives. Katz (1985) mentioned that the new employee must create a cognitive or mental map of the organizational surroundings and cast of the characters in the work environment.

During this period the new employee must complete three important tasks: building an organizational role identity, learning about new superiors and other employees, and deciphering the reward system and organizational norms. Intervention strategies must be evolved by the practitioners through which new the employee could be effectively socialized in its "breaking in" phase and learn the three socialization tasks proposed by Katz. Human resource practitioners should plan and facilitate orientation programmes aimed at ensuring successful socialization into organizations (Jackson, 1984).

Anticipatory socialization programme proposed by Kramer (1974) includes the stress management interventions for new employees. This program is based on the assumption that stress results from the gap between the expectations the new employees have and the reality of the jobs, they encounter. The programme includes following four phases:

(1) Participants are presented with real life incidents that the new worker might encounter on the job.

(2) Participants are asked what they could do to offer alternative solutions if the impossible conditions exist.

(3) Participants are allowed to gain a 'realistic baseline' of expectations by exposing them to a panel of workers whom they would encounter in the field.

(4) Participants are taught theories and techniques of conflict resolution and negotiation.

***Improving Organizational Structure and Climate*:** Structure and climate of the organization largely influence job behaviour of its members as well as its overall effectiveness. A variety of job stress can be easily prevented or mitigated by improving organizational structure and creating a congenial climate in the organization. Ross and Altmaier (1994) have mentioned three intervention strategies for dealing with stress arising from inadequate organization structure and climate: decentralization, participative decision making and climate survey.

***Decentralization*:** The organizations with high centralization of power or authority are likely to cause more stress to its members. Strategies for promoting decentralization within organizations have become increasingly popular in recent years. Schuler and Sethi (1984) have suggested changing communication patterns and networks within organizations and developing work groups as the effective techniques of decentralization. It was noted that in a autonomous work group wherein the team had control of pace of their work, rest breaks, and allocation of work assignments showed better task identity development and less emotional distress among the workers (Wall & Clegg, 1981).

Participative Decision Making: Another intervention strategy is participative decision making. It is also related to decentralization and involves creating systems and communication channels in the organization in such a manner that employees of all levels are involved in making important decisions. Being involved in the process of decision making employees feel a greater sense of influence and control, and so experience lesser ambiguity and distress. Moreover, finding ways in which the worker can influence the job demands, decreases the likelihood of experience of role conflicts (Murphy, 1984). The effectiveness of the participative decision making intervention would depend upon two conditions: (i) management should be committed to the philosophy of participative decision making and (ii) the kind of decisions that are offered for employees participation. Employees would be most interested in decisions on those matters which are important or relevant to them (Ivancevich & Matteson, 1980). Employees will feel that they have some say only if they are asked to offer salient input on issues that affect their daily work.

Climate Survey: Third organizational structure improvement method associated with stress management concerns the use of climate survey. This intervention is also known as attitude survey, opinion survey, or employee reaction surveys. These surveys are designed to elicit employees reactions and preferences to help management in developing strategies that might improve organizational effectiveness and employees' satisfaction. Management identifies the inadequate and non-congenial aspects of organizational climate and makes possible effort to offer feedback.

Career Planning and Management: A number of stressors have been identified for the employees as they move beyond the period when they enter the workplace. These stressors are related to the mid-career development of employees. Ross and Altmaier (1994) have suggested evolving intervention strategies which help in avoiding the stresses employees experience in course of their career development. Today a more advanced conceptualization of career development is needed because of the drastic changes taking place, such as structural changes within organizations, demographic changes in the workforce, changes in the nature of work with rapidly advancing technology. In view of the present changes, new and creative intervention strategies would be required in helping employees to deal with career development stresses. However, Kaye (1982) has suggested the advantages of career development intervention strategies, such as increased employee skill building, improved talent matching, individual revitalization, problem identification, and increased goal commitment. Some programmes in this direction are integration of organizational needs into career planning system, helping employees understand the value of lateral waves, identify skills that transfer among job families, take initiative in making career contacts, and use the company job position system.

Hall (1986) has presented a useful model in understanding the interventions in the stresses associated with career development. He explains career development as being comprised of two components: career planning and career management. Career management is the responsibility of the organization and includes employees' selection, training, job rotation, performance appraisal, and promotion. Career planning is the responsibility of the employee and involves the activities of self-assessment, career choice, choice of organization, prep-aration of career plan and monitoring career opportunities. The practitioner can help combating stress by focusing individuals on those career activities within their control. Through seminar, testing, individual counselling, a practitioner can assist the employee for being cautious and active about their career and life planning to taking more active role in these activities.

Pestonjee and Muncherji (1991) have also discussed about the relationship between career paths and health of executives and suggested the ways to avoid stress and strains caused from career development. Crucial points in career development occur at key times during the individuals life, i.e., at about the age of thirty, during forties, and again in late fifties. Each career stage is characterized by different issues and problems. Career management programmes to help employees cope with the problems arising out of career development should be run by the HRD department of the organizations. These programmes vary greatly in scope and content, but most of them involve efforts to (1) help employees assess their own career strengths, (2) set priorities and specific career goals, (3) provide information on different career paths and alternatives within the organization, and (4) offer employees yearly reviews of their progress towards these goals by managers. In addition, special workshops and technical training opportunities are often parts of such programmes.

Pestonjee and Muncherji (1991) have also suggested intervention strategies for those employees also who are on the verge of their retirement. This involves a gradual reorientation away from their careers and work toward leisure time activities. It requires careful planning to meet the special challenges faced by retired workers such as a loss of status, reduced earning, reduced feeling of accomplishment, and a loss of social relations. The employee should try to take a practical view of these major changes and try to adjust to them. The organizations should also try to re-employ a few of capable individuals. Special training programmes on post superanuation phase of the career are also vital.

Stress Audit: Pestonjee (1992) has suggested "Stress Audit" as a proactive intervention which an organization can adopt to manage stress of managerial personnel. When an organization decides to have a scientific look at the mental-cum-physical health status of its executives, it is called a stress audit. A stress audit refers to the attempt an organization makes to study, explore and control the various types of stress which the executives experience. In stress audit systematic study is made of the dominant stressors prevalent in the organization, its divisions and departments. A stress audit includes collection of data pertaining to organizational climate, role stress, job satisfaction, job analysis, etc.

5

ELIMINATING OR MITIGATING ORGANIZATIONAL STRESSORS

Although stress of certain type and to some extent can be prevented at an individual and organizational level, it is impossible to make the work environment entirely free from all sorts of stresses. Stress is an inevitable part of a job. However, some existing stressors can be eliminated, and the frequency as well as severity of the job stressors can be mitigated to some extent by putting into effect various corrective interventions by the management as well as by individual employees.

A number of stress researchers (Caplan, et al., 1975; Cooper & Marshall, 1976; French & Caplan, 1972; Kahn & Quinn, 1970) have alluded to the significant role organizations can play in reducing the courses of stress in their environment. Organizations might begin by surveying their environment and identifying the positions, conditions and events which are potential sources of stress for their employees. This knowledge could then be used to orchestrate a better person-environment fit, both through changes in the established organizational structure, policies and procedure, and through introduction of a wide range of stress management programmes. The former might be seen in such moves as decentralization, resource distribution and alteration of reward procedures.

Recognizing that considerable stress can be generated by interpersonal interactions demanded in managerial roles, organizations can choose to focus some of their interventions directly on the work unit. Identifying specific stress creating situations within the group and improving group functioning through programmes in the areas of communication skill, team-building, developing support networks, participative problem solving and decision-making are some of the ways of mitigating the level of organizational stress and improving employees' quality of coping. A variety of corrective interventions can be put into effect to eliminate or minimize the situations of job stress, such as transferring individuals into roles, allowing a better person-environment fit, changing or shifting role functions, identifying limitations in skill areas, and giving access to skill training, to examining the work-family interface in relation to individual's specific role demands.

Cooper and Marshall (1976) have extended certain suggestions to reduce managerial stress. They argued that understanding the sources of managerial pressures is itself the first step in stress reduction. Next, we must begin to explore 'when' and 'how' to intervene. There are a number of changes that can be introduced in organizational life to begin to mitigate stress at work, for example:

(1) To recreate the social, psychological, and organizational environment in the workplace, to encourage greater autonomy and participation by managers in their jobs.

(2) To build the bridges between the workplace and the home.

(3) To utilize the well-developed catalogue of social and interactive skills, training programmes to help clarify role and to understand and resolve the difficulties relating to interpersonal relationships within organizations.

(4) And more fundamentally, to create an organizational climate to encourage communication, openness, and trust so that the individual managers are able to express their inability to cope, with their work related fears, and are able to ask for help, if needed.

Job Characteristics Approach to Reduce Stress

Agrawal (1984) suggested for application of 'Job Characteristics Approach' in preventing or mitigating organizational stress. He argued that organizational stress can be well managed by creating a fit between person and his job. This congruence between the two can be attained by properly designing the task in accordance with the characteristics of the individual who has to perform that task. Agrawal noted that job characteristics approach may be of great help in reducing job stress in the following ways:

(1) In repetitive tasks, the activation level of the individual falls below the characteristic norms. As a result of it he experiences negative effects and tries to increase the activation level by increasing the degree of impact of job on him. In case he is prevented from increasing the level of job impact, his performance level goes down, and consequently he experiences stress. By introducing variations in repetitive tasks employees' performance level can be increased and his stress can be reduced.

(2) Task autonomy, which includes freedom, independence and discretion in scheduling work, has been found to increase employees' overall job satisfaction and to reduce their boredom, monotony, irritation and restlessness. Agrawal inferred that the extent to which the job characteristic model provides the opportunity to satisfy employees autonomy needs, enhances his job satisfaction and reduces his stress.

(3) Agrawal has noted that task feedback is perceived as the most accurate source of feedback particularly because it is difficult to measure the performance of others. Task feedback, therefore, is perceived as evoking self-evaluation and increasing intrinsic motivation in the employee to the maximum extent.

Reducing Job Stress Though Participative Job Characteristics Model

Agrawal (1984) has suggested this approach to job characteristics model benefitted from the principles of socio-technical design (Cherns, 1976) and action research perspective (Lewin, 1951). In socio-technical design the need of a constructive participative organization has been emphasized in order to make the system capable of self-modernization, adaptive to change, and effective in making proper use of the manpower. The only condition for this is that people should be given the opportunity to participate in the designing of the job they are to perform. Moreover, the action research perspective suggests that data derive their meaning in a 'given context' and hence, the client system should be involved in interpreting and analyzing the data. By using this participative approach, organizational stress can be reduced to a great extent. The author has suggested following advantages of his new model which help in preventing or reducing organizational stress:

(a) congruence between job and individual characteristics,
(b) role clarity,
(c) increase in expectancy (effort-performance),
(d) increase in expectancy (performance-reward),
(e) control of organizational stress,
(f) enhancement in productivity,
(g) enhancement in workers' satisfaction, and decrement in the rate of absenteeism and turnover.

Bhandarker and Singh (1986) while studying the entire stress cycle, evolved an action plan for reducing managerial stress. They proposed the triprobed action plan aimed at three levels, namely, individual, organizational and societal level. At organizational level, stress can be reduced by:

(1) helping them to reduce friction between work and home life at a minimal,
(2) improving channels of communication; sharing information and greater feedback on performance to develop one's sense of identity in the system,

(3) giving greater assurance to management and support to reduce psychological burden,
(4) facilitating greater intercadre relationship among employees to build positive relationship,
(5) using demographic information to identify stress prone persons,
(6) introducing compulsory breathing exercises,
(7) improving health related facilities, and
(8) making annual holidays compulsory.

At the societal level, individual stress can be reduced by:

(1) teaching belief in self through facilitating independence with the environment,
(2) a larger movement to discourage mindless pill-popping, and
(3) shifting focus to Indian heritage for the sake of suitable habits and life pattern.

Reducing Stress by Job Redesign and Enrichment

Ross and Altmaier (1994) suggest that occupational stress can be reduced or moderated by improving job characteristic through job redesign technique. An important intervention strategy might be to seek ways to train managers and engineer personnel in the area of job design. The human resource practitioner should recognize the stresses arising from job task, operation of other stressors, indicators of stress, and coping process and redesign the job and improve the job characteristics to reduce or moderate the prevailing stressors. Job redesign involves changing certain aspects of the task which might lead to improved efficiency or effectiveness in work. The important starting points for this intervention is a complete and thorough understanding of the job, creativity of the supervisor, employee and consultant which determine the effective intervention to be developed and applied.

Job enrichment is a subset of job redesign interventions. These strategies are described as restructuring of a job to make it more meaningful, challenging, and intrinsically rewarding (Matteson & Ivancevich, 1987). Job enrichment leads to an increase in job related activities, responsibilities, autonomy, skills-required or a combination of them which, in turn, necessitate an increase in monetary gain of the employees. The lack of a contingent reward system may arouse feelings of unequality among workers because they expect that an enriched job would lead to more promotions and higher salary. Agrawal has reported that contingent reward helps in avoiding conflicts and moderating the stress in work enrichment. Another strategy of this intervention is to enhance the job involvement and intrinsic motivation of the employee through job enlargement technique. In this strategy some more duties and responsibilities are added to the present job role without withdrawing any existing responsibilities. But this enlargement of the job must be within a convenient level so that it does not cause role overload, ambiguities and conflicts. Kopleman (1986) found in his study that job enrichment programmes significantly reduced workers' stress and improved the quantity of the product. However, quantity was unaffected by the introduction of job enrichment. Besides the quantitative and qualitative nature of work, the practitioner might also consider enriching jobs in terms of their core job features. These features include autonomy, feedback, skill variance, task identity and task significance. But it is important here to take care of the individual difference in this context.

The extent to which different employees will find these task attributes rewarding will vary greatly, thus managers should consider how they can communicate effectively with their employees. Another important intervention in occupational stress in this category is scheduling the work hours. This scheduling may be of three types: compressed work week, flextime, and job sharing. In "compressed work week" the worker may be allowed to increase the hours of work per day and reduce the days in a week, the worker may like to work for 10 hours a day per week. Another type of scheduling, i.e., "flextime", may allow the worker to vary their work schedule within prescribed limits. In "job sharing" an employee may share his job responsibilities on one full-time job with another employee. Effectiveness of these scheduling have been established by some researchers. It was noted that greater flexibility and discretion in schedule was correlated with decreased absenteeism, better performance, and fewer psychological symptoms among the workers. These effects seem to be related to the degree of control a worker feels is available when scheduling is flexible (Pierce & Newstorm, 1983). Schuler and Sethi (1984) argued that discretion in scheduling allows the workers to fulfill the obligations and responsibilities they have off-the-job. In order to reduce the stress caused from monotony, provision for periodical change in employees' duties should be made. This intervention can prevent the experience of stress and burnout of the employee from this prolonged engagement in highly demanding and strenuous tasks. Instead of single man responsibility, joint responsibility can reduce the stress of the jobs involving work overload and crucial decisions.

Setting the Goals

Role ambiguity and role confusion are the major sources of occupational stress. But by setting goals these problems could be resolved to a great extent. Goal setting involves determining specific standards of performance for the workers. According to Locke and Latham (1984) goal setting reduces stress in four ways:

(i) the employee receives a sense of satisfaction when a goal is achieved,

(ii) the process of being involved in individual action can be reassuring,

(iii) the goal setting process gives the employee a sense of continuous moving towards the set goal, and

(iv) goal setting reduces the feeling of uncertainty that an employee might experience with regard to evaluation of his performance. The set goal must be challenging but not too difficult.

Management by objectives (MBO) developed by Druker (1954) is a well-known system of goal setting. MBO starts a mission statement that defines the group's purpose. MBO is based upon two philosophical assumptions: (1) participation in goal setting increases motivation and ego involvement; and (2) participative goal setting fastens self-control and reduces the need for external control. In MBO the actions to be achieved and the process of monitoring progress are clearly defined before performance begins. Goals and series of action steps or objectives are also planned in advance. MBO minimizes job stress by avoiding ambiguities and conflicts in role, and providing feedback concerning the individual's efforts towards goal-achievement. It also mitigates the stress and moderates strains of role overload through the positive feeling generated by participation, cooperative efforts, and ego involvement in the organizational goals.

Performance Feedback

It has been well recognized that feedback on performance affects motivation and satisfaction. It has been noted that, lack of feedback or faulty evaluation leads to stress. Not only are these systems, linked to stress, but they are closely associated with burnout (Jackson, 1984). Interventions should be evolved to give proper feedback to the workers. The supervisors must be trained for performance appraisal and to communicate employees about their performance in behaviourally specific terms. The supervisor must obtain rating information about the workers' performance from different and objective sources. The evaluation of the performance may be made on the basis of the ratings obtaining from customers or clients and co-workers. Workers may be also allowed to give feedback to each other.

Team-Building Interventions

Overall competence of an organization largely depends on the ability of its members to work effectively in teams. This has more relevance in recent times when organizations must deal with increasingly complex technological problems that can no longer be handled by single individuals. Thus, improving the effectiveness of various teams within organizations is one of the most important functions being performed by organizational development specialists. "Team feeling", in addition to improving organizational effectiveness, prevents and mitigates the stresses of job life. Some of the interventions for team-building are directed at special groups, such as temporary teams created to tackle specific tasks, *ad hoc* committees, and newly formed groups. The interventions are usually focused on one or more of the following objectives: (i) analyzing and clarifying role expectation and obligations of team members; (ii) improving superior-subordinate or peer relations; (iii) improving problem solving, decision making, resource utilization, or planning activities; (iv) reducing conflicts; and (v) improving organizational climate.

The role analysis intervention consists of a structured series of meetings in which each individual lists the specific duties and responsibilities of the job with the help of peers, lists what is expected from others, learns what others expect from the individual, and leaves the programme with a written summary of his or her complete team role. The family group in its meetings discuss and diagnose the problems and its causes. The group generate preliminary action steps for improving team effectiveness by deciding upon the action steps to be taken. The team also ensures that the intended changes take place and remain stable over time.

Managerial Interventions for Stress Management

Ivancevich and Matteson (1987) have suggested certain managerial actions which may be developed and implemented to prevent and reduce the stresses of job life. Specific managerial interventions should be made to prevent or reduce the stresses which emerge in context of five organizational level targets for managerial action, namely, intrinsic job, organizational structure and culture, reward systems, human resorce systems, leadership systems. Table 5.1 lists some potential organizational strategies that practitioners could incorportate in combating stress.

Table 5.1
Organizational Stressors and Managerial Interventions

Context	*Stressor*	*Managerial Action*
Intrinsic to job	Work overload	Redesign job to match individual's skills, energy, needs.
Intrinsic to job	Insufficient control of resources	Initiate, through participation, involvement, and discretion in job related events.
Organizational structure and culture	Red tape	Simplify relationships between levels in the hierarchy.
Organizational structure and culture	Lack of mission and strategy	Circulate the mission and strategy being used by the company, department or unit.
Reward systems	Inequitable rewards	Conduct survey to determine points of concern and correct problems that can be reasonably changed.
Human resource systems	Lack of training	Institute training programs that can improve self-confidence, and performance.
Human resource systems	Lack of job security	Provide job security to the possible extents.
Leadership systems	Poor relationship	Institute team building programme that would involve leaders and followers.
Leadership System	Lack of respect	Improve selection process for hiring or promoting leaders so that most talented individuals hold these positions.

Role Efficacy as Stress Reducer

Role based stress not only affects pleasantness at work but also reduces one's potentiality to perform effectively. Pareek (1987, 1993) has proposed the concept of 'role efficacy' and advocated that if organizations assist employees to define their roles and if they are willing to share this concern through strategies, such as proactivity, conrontation, developing helping relationships and creativity, then it is possible to reduce role based strains. This is possible as a result of an individual's movement from a reactive role taking behaviour to a proactive role making behaviour. Pareek (1993) Table 5.2 classified different aspects or dimensions of role efficacy into three groups, namely, role making, role centering, and role linking. The first dimension is of role making which is active attitude towards the. role (to define and make the role as one likes). It is the opposite to role taking where the person mainly responds to other's expectations with a passive attitude. The second dimension is of role centering which refers to the significance of role in the organization. The role must provide an opportunity to satisfy the needs for power, control, and personal growth. Third dimension, role linking, involves inter-role linkage and helping relationship. These three dimensions of role efficacy can be achieved by integrating certain specific features in the structure of roles, which could prevent role stress as well as enhance role efficiency of the employees.

Table 5.2
Dimensions of Role Efficacy and Its Components.

Dimension 1

Role Making	:	Taking initiative in role designing.
Components		
Self-role integration	:	Integration between self-con cept and role demands
Pro-activity	:	Initiating action.
Creativity :		Trying new ideas or strategies.
Conforntation	:	Facing problems.

Dimension 2

Role Centering	:	Establishing importance of role in the system.
Components		
Centrality	:	Feeling important and central in the system.
Influence	:	Feeling that role can make some impact on the system.
Growth	:	Feeling that role would provide opportu-nity for personal growth.
Dimension 3		
Linking	:	Linking with other roles and people.
Components		
Inter-role linkage	:	Linking of one role with other roles.
Helping relationships	:	Giving and receiving help amongst roles.
Super-ordination	:	Linkage of one's role with a larger entity or cause.

Sayeed (1985a) in his study noted that individual's role making or proactive behaviour is greatly affected by the degree of experienced tension on the job. He emphasized role intervention strategies to enhance individual role efficacy, so that an individual could relate with the organization in the role capacity as effectively as possible. This, in turn, would reduce the stressful situations in the organization.

Conversion of Burnout Situation into Glow up Situation

Burnout is an extreme state of the focal person as a consequence of consistent high level of job stress, representing major personal, organizational and social costs. But by using appropriate strategies the situation of burnout can be avoided or at least moderated to a considerable extent. Pareek (1982) has suggested that the burnout situation can be converted in glow up situation using appropriate strategies and interventions at individual and organization level (Figure 5.1). The model presents how the stress-arousing characteristics of personal, organizational and behavioural factors/ situations can be converted into stress-resistant or stress reducing characteristics leading to a glow up situation.

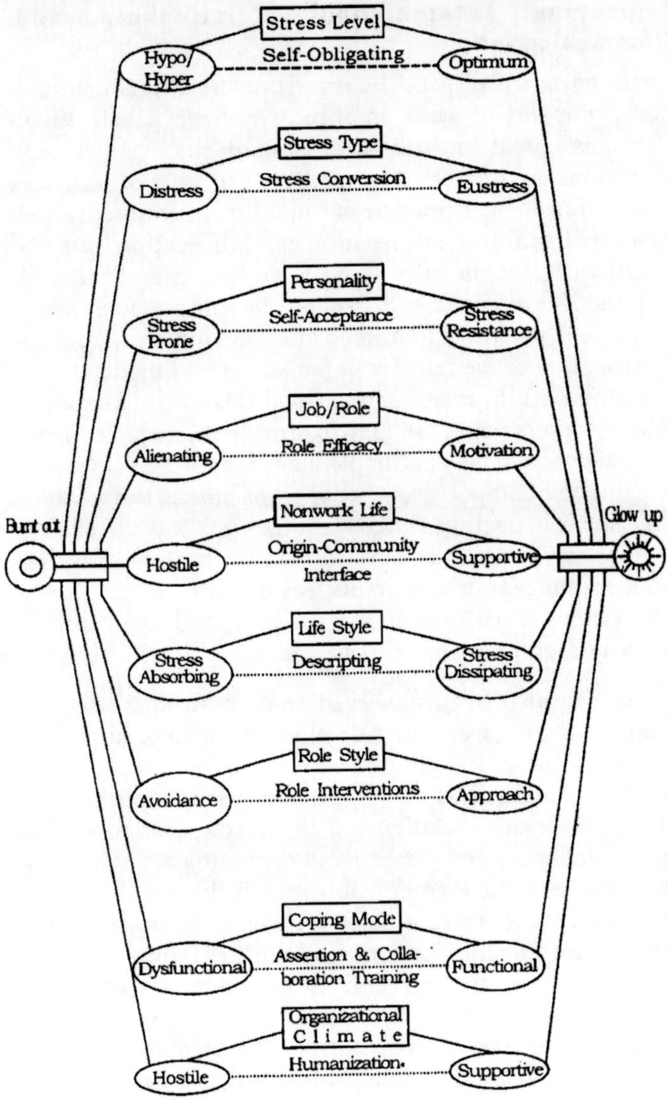

Fig. 5.1 Executive Glow up and Burnout: Contributing Factors and Conversion Strategies

Note : Dotted lines show conversion strategies.

Source : Pareek U. (1982), Executive Glow up and Burnout. (Mimeo). Ahmedabad : Indian Institute of Management.

Improving Interpersonal Relationship and Communication

Importance of good interpersonal relationships and social support at work has been well recognized. But it becomes a great source of stress if inadequate or strained. The relationships that exist between co-workers are characterized by the nature of communication. Proper and smooth intra-and inter-cadre communication provide emotional attachment, enhances 'we feeling' and 'morale', and reduces stress as well. Feeling of social support among employees generated from good interpersonal relationships is also an effective reducer of job stress and moderator of the stress-strain relationship. Good relationship between fellow workers might function to provide emotional support or to offer actual help in completing some job. The managers seeking to build positive relationships among the workers and, in turn, decrease stress, should seek ways to ensure the two-way communication. The manager must hold regular staff meetings in which employees could talk about their frustrations at work and outside the work, and about specific work-related problems and issues.

It has also been observed that more and effective communication from the side of supervisors or superiors decrease the probability of experience of stress by the workers. Communication is an important component in the interpersonal relationship that occurs at work. The more managers and supervisors communicate effectively with workers, the greater will be the likelihood of workers to experience less stress. Good interpersonal relationships and proper communication generate the feeling of social support among the workers, which moderate the stress as well as buffers the consequent strains. Schuler and Sethi (1984) have noted that educating managers and supervisors to build communication skill is an intervention in management of occupational stress. Ross and Altmair (1994) have mentioned types of managerial communication behaviour which help in reducing employees' stress as shorwn in Table 5.3.

Table 5.3
Managerial Communication Behaviour for Stress Reduction

Communication Behaviour	*Example*
Achievement	Conveys statement of goals, challenge, confidence and high expectation.
Contingent approval	Aid employee in knowing what is expected. Managers communicate contingent approval by praising employees good performance.
Directive	Offers direction or guidance when the employee wants it.
Supportive	Indicates concern for the employee as a person.
Ego deflation	Reverse of achievement communication behaviour.
Contringent disapproval	Let the employee know which behavioure will be punished or not rewarded. Give employee direction for future behaviour.
Contingent disapproval	Let the employee know which behaviours will be punished or not rewarded. Give employee direction for future behaviour.
Participative	Helps employees in setting future goals, and direction on how to do a job best. Reduces conflicts between supervisors and employee.

6
COPING WITH OCCUPATIONAL STRESS

Coping has long been ascribed as a central role in human adaptation. People ultimately adopt one or another sort of adaptive behaviour in order to deal with the confronting situations of stress. Sometimes they make even spontaneous responses to adjust with the situation of stress at subconscious level. These specific efforts made by the stressed person are denoted as coping behaviour. Biologists use the term coping to refer to the adjustment of a tissue system or the body to noxious agents as in Selye' (1956, 1976) "General Adaptation Syndrome". However, coping is primarily a psychological concept. The coping process in its broadest sense refers to any attempt to deal with stressful situation which a person feels he must do something about, but which tax or exceed his existing adaptation response patterns. Coping behaviours can range from the most casual manoeuvres to complicated forms of problem solving, from most highly proactive behaviour to the most pathological reactive attempts and from most rational to the most irrational efforts. Yet, all are undertaken with the same ultimate objectives of preventing, reducing or resolving the stress and its consequences. Lazarus and Folkman (1984) have defined coping at the psychological level of analysis as "the process of managing (mastering, tolerating or reducing) external or internal demands that are appraised as taxing or exceeding the resources of the person". The definition has several important functions. First, it emphasizes "process" as distinguished from trait or style. Second, it speaks of "management" rather than mastery. Third, the term "appraisal" indicates the central role of psychological mediation. Finally, the coping has been viewed as entailing the mobilization of effort. The ultimate function of the coping is to get relief from the pressure of the feeling of stress to the focal person. Muhanic (1974) has cited three functions of effective coping: dealing with social and environmental demands, having the motivation to meet with such demands, and maintaining a state of psychological equilibrium in order to direct energy and skill toward meeting external demands. Pearlin and Schooler (1978) likewise identified three functions of coping: changing the situation out of which stressful experience arises, controlling the meaning of such experiences before they become stressful, and controlling stress itself after it has been generated. Cohen and Lazarus (1979) suggested five main coping tasks: (i) to reduce harmful environmental conditions and enhance prospects of recovery, (ii) to tolerate or adjust to negative events and realities, (iii) to maintain a positive self-image, (iv) to maintain emotional equilibrium, and (v) to continue satisfying relationships with others.

Coping Strategies

In fact common to all these coping tasks is a distinction of overriding importance between "problem-focused" and "emotion focused" coping (Cohen & Lazarus, 1979; Folkman, 1982; Folkman & Lazarus, 1980). Problem-focused coping strategies refer to efforts directed at doing something constructive about the conditions that cause stress. Emotion-focused coping refers to efforts directed at regulating the emotion itself. The two modes of coping have differential effect on mental health of the focal person. The researchers have obtained clear evidence that most people use both modes of coping in daily stressful encounters. However, it has now been proved that responses made in order to cope with stresses form several factors rather than just two (Aldwin & Revenson, 1987; Folkman & Lazarus, 1985; Scheier et al, 1986). These factors often diverge quite sharply in character, to the extent being inversely correlated.

Pareek (1983b) has proposed two styles of coping which people generally adopt in order to deal with perceived stress, i.e., functional and dysfunctional. In functional coping style the focal person confronts and makes some efforts to deal with stressful situations. This style may also be referred to as "approach" made of coping. In dysfunctional mode of coping the individual denies the stress or tries to escape from it. This style is denoted as "avoidance" mode of coping. Combining the source of stress (i.e. expressing aggression toward himself or aggression and blame on the external factors) and mode of coping (i.e. approach and avoidance), Pareek has suggested four approach and four avoidance coping strategies which people adopt in their every day lives. Approach coping strategies are: impersistive, intropersistive, extrapersistive, and interpersistive. Avoidance coping strategies are: impunitive, intropunitive, extrapunitive, and defensive. Briefly these coping strategies may be described as under:

Approach Coping Strategies

Impersistive: This strategy is characterized by low internality low externality and approach. Individual hopes that time or normally expected circumstances will bring about the solution of the problem.

Intropersistive: It is characterized by high internality, low externality and approach. Individual himself takes action in relation to the faced stress.

Extrapersistive: It is characterized by low internality, high externality and approach. In this strategy the individual requests someone to solve the problem or expects that the solution will come from other people.

Interpersistive: It is characterized by high internality, high externality and approach. Herein, the individual makes joint efforts with others to deal with stress.

Avoidance Coping Strategies

Impunitive: It has combination of low internality, low externality and avoidance. Herein the individual blames others for the stress situation and simply admits stress as an unavoidable situation with a belief that nothing can be done about it.

Intropunitive: It is a combination of high internality, low externality and avoidance. Herein the individual directs the blame and aggression to himself.

Extrapunitive: It is characterized by low internality, high externality and avoidance. In this strategy the individual expresses irritation and aggression towards external factors, and blames others for creating stress.

Defensive: It is characterized by high internality, high externality and avoidance. In this strategy the focal person either denies the stress or gives rationalization to the stressful situation in order to defend his superego.

There is no clear consensus as to which of the various coping modes is most effective. The effectiveness of a coping strategy largely depends upon the nature and severity of the perceived stress and other situational factors. However, in his study on a sample of industrial employees, Srivastava and Singh (1987) noted that though the employees who adopted "approach" coping strategies experienced comparatively more stress, but indicated to maintain better mental health. The study also revealed that employees who perceived job stress as being resulted from external environment and adopted approach coping strategies, maintained better mental health in comparison to those who attributed the stress to internal factors (personal characteristics). Approach mode of coping has also been noted to buffer the inverse relationship between job stress and mental health of the employees. Out of the above discussion it may be concluded that for effective dealing with stress "one should generally adopt approach modes of coping wherein one makes realistic appraisal of the stress, and makes all possible efforts with optimistic attitude to deal with the situation of stress".

Folkman et al. (1986) have suggested eight types of coping strategies, i.e., confronting, distancing, self-control, seeking social support, accepting responsibility, escaping, planned problem solving, and positive reappraisal. Wilder and Pluchik (1982) have also suggested eight types of coping responses, namely: suppression, help seeking, replacement (engaging in direct stress-reducing activities), blaming others or the system, substitution (engaging in indirect stress-reducing activities), mapping (collecting more information), reversal (acting opposite to the way one feels), and minimization.

Carver, Weintraub, and Seheier (1989) have developed a multidimensional coping inventory, which include fourteen coping strategies, such as—active coping, planning, suppression of competitive activities, restraint coping, seeking social support (instrumental), seeking social support (emotional), positive reinterpretation and growth, acceptance, turning to religion, focus on and venting of emotions, denial, behavioural disengagement, mental disengagement, and alcohol and drug abuse.

Newton and Keenan (1985) have identified six categories of coping strategies adopted by the employees to deal with their stresses of job life. These strategies are—talk to others, direct action toward solution of the problem, preparatory action (problem appraisal, getting information, and seeking alternative methods of solution), withdrawal, feeling helpless and expressing resentment and other categories (conform to superior's expression, and show assertiveness to others). These researchers concluded that coping strategies cannot be identified as universally effective. It was also noted that choice of specific coping strategy to deal with a stress situation is determined by the individual and environmental characteristics, but not by the subjective appraisal of the stressors.

Latack (1984, 1986) suggested three categories of coping strategies, namely, action coping, cognitive reappraisal, and symptom management. Action is focused on one's cognitions of situation, and symptom management. The strategies that Folkman and Lazarus (1980) have labelled as "emotion-focused" are more precisely viewed as cognitive reappraisal because these coping strategies are most immediately and directly aimed at changing thoughts about the situation. Indirectly they may influence psycho-physiological distress, but the initial target is revision of the cognitive appraisal itself. Thus, the first two categories, action and cognitive reappraisal, correspond to problem-focused and emotion-focused coping, respectively. Symptom management strategies are thought of as emotional-physical in focus. These strategies are brought into play on a more global level. Latak has further classified both action and cognitive strategies into 'control' and 'escape'. 'Control', consisting of both action and cognitive reappraisals that are proactive, take-charge in tone. 'Escape' consists of both actions and cognitive reappraisals that suggest an escapist or avoidance mode.

Latak (1986) examined the relationship of these strategies, adopted by the employees, in coping with job stress arising from role conflicts, role ambiguity and role overload, to their job satisfaction and severity of stress symptoms. The results indicated that 'control' coping strategies were correlated positively with job satisfaction and negatively with anxiety and psychosomatic symptoms, whereas 'escape' coping strategies were found to be correlated negatively with job satisfaction and positively with stress symptoms. The symptom management strategies correlated positively with stress symptoms.

Ways of Handling Tension used by Executives

A series of investigations have examined the use of various types of coping behaviour by individuals in a work setting. Mann (unpublished manuscript) identified following ways in which executives handle the tension and pressures of their jobs and maintain their well-being: (1) withdraw physically from the situation temporarily, (2) change to a different task or job activity, (3) change to an engrossing non-work activity, (4) modify focus of attention, (5) analyze the situation and change strategy of attach, (6) engage in physical exercise, (7) aggress and ventilate feelings, (8) use different types of sedation, (9) talk through with spouse, (10) talk through with other, (11) seek help of God, (12) build body resistance to frustrations, and (13) compartmentalize work and home life.

Table 6.1 give is a list of some effective coping strategies proposed in the popular literature to deal with the stresses of job life.

Table 6.1
Strategies for Coping with Job Stress

Coping Strategy	*Proponent*
Build work-group norms of cooperation not competition.	Chase (1972), DeVille (1970)
Delegate, seek help of others.	DeVille (1970), Fair (1976)
Building satisfactory relationship with supervisor.	DeVille (1970)
Plan instead of responding to pressure.	Howard (1978)
Divert attention from stressful situation.	Uris (1972)
Self-awareness what causes you stress, how do you respond to stress.	Overbeke (1975), Student (1975, 1977), Fair (1976)
Take vacation and holiday time.	Walsh (1975), Uris (1970)
Devote yourself fully to what you are doing.	Bensahel (1974)
Problem solving, planning, pacing of one's working day.	Fair (1976)
Do one thing at a time.	Bensahel (1974)
Develop perspective recognize the inevitable.	Overbeke (1975), Student (1977) Bensahel (1974)
Relaxation	Benson (1974), Marks and Banack (1977)
Compartmentalize work and home life.	Marks & Banack (1977)
Develop interpersonal skill, consideration for others.	Chase (1972)
Work smarter not harder.	Howard, Rechnitzer, and Cunningham (1975)
Promise yourself a reward when situation of stress is over.	Bensahel (1974)

Coping with Role Stress

It has been a general observation that job role causes maximum stress to the executive. But this stress can be effectively dealt with through various coping strategies. In this pursuit, Pestonjee (1992) has suggested some specific skills and coping strategies which could be quite effective in dealing with different types of role stress experienced by the executives. Table 6.2 depicts the variety of role stress and coping skills and strategies to deal with them.

Table 6.2
Role Stress and Coping Skills and Strategies

Sources of Role Stress	*Coping Skills and Strategies*
1. Role ambiguity (feedback).	Defining one's goal clearly in view of the organizational goal.
2. Role ambiguity (task)	Be more proactive than reactive; ask for information from superiors, subordinates and colleagues.
3. Person-role conflict	Re-clarify and increase the ability to integrate one's values with others; discriminate between legitimate and illegitimate expectations held by others.
4. Inter-role conflict	Setting up limits on demands of each roles; weighting one demand against the other.
5. Role-conflict (inter-sender)	Ability to look for possible consequences before taking a decision; ability to disintegrate view points, etc.
6. Role-overload	Ability to set priorities; increase one's assertiveness; better time management skill; self-delegation.
7. Personal inadequacy	Identifying and developing technical and managerial skills required.
8. Resource inadequacy	Ability to manage with existing resources; accepting task conditionally; realizing one's limitations.

9. Role shrinkage	Ask for new tasks; develop specialized skills to become a specialist.
10. Role isolation	Involve others in decision-making; develop participative managerial skills.
11. Role stagnation	Ask for a change in role; delegate obsolete duties and tasks; start training one's subordinates.

Sam Batlivala (1990) in his study found that Indian executives adopted following coping strategies to deal with their job stresses:

1. Critical analysis and recognizing problems
2. Yoga
3. Practicing good management
4. Sexs
5. If underreward, slow down and work in proportion to output
6. Talking to the boss/union
7. Improving self-image
8. Unwinding and going on vacation
9. Overvaluing outcome of others
10. Overvaluing own inputs
11. Maintaining better family relationships
12. Using scientific methods
13. Being decisive
14. Acquiring alternative interests or starting other business
15. Avoiding confrontation
16. Developing trust in ownself
17. Acquiring more qualifications
18. Using better communication
19. Decreasing own reward
20. If overreward, increase output
21. Changing the person to whom comparing ownself
22. Undervalue output
23. Resignation

There might be many other coping strategies which

employees would be using to deal with their job stresses is accordance with the nature of stress situation, available physical resources, and their own personal resources and characteristics. But generalization cannot be made about the extent of effectiveness of various coping strategies. It would not be appropriate to say as to which is the best or universally effective coping strategy. The effectiveness of a coping strategy depends upon the nature of the stress situation and several other co-existing situational variables. Coping is actually a dynamic process. Lazarus (1980) concluded that effectiveness of coping strategies depends upon controllability of the situation. Different coping strategies can vary in primacy across the time for an employee, and more than one or even contrary modes of coping may be adopted to deal with a situation of stress at work. The employee may use cognitive as well as combative (action oriented) strategies at the same time. It is also a possibility that the employee adopts the approach mode of coping for one part of the situation and avoidance coping strategy to effectively deal with the rest part of that situations of stress. In certain situation avoidance coping strategies might prove more effective and useful than the approach coping strategies.

Thus, use of various coping strategies can be evaluated separately as they interact in terms of a variety of consequences relevant to coping effectiveness. However, among the ineffective coping behaviours are those which might work in the short run but not in the long run, and those which appear to work but at the cost of employees' morale, performance and health. To conclude, it may be suggested that psychological well-being of the employees as well as effectiveness of the organization must be taken into consideration while making any effort toward management of organizational stress. The employees may be trained or suggested to use most suitable coping strategies in the framework of the nature of stressful situation, available resources, context of the situation, and the ultimate outcomes.

7

MODERATING OCCUPATIONAL STRESS AND STRAINS

Next step toward management of stress is to moderate the severity of inevitable stress and consequent strains. Stress of certain type sometimes becomes unavoidable or beyond control. In such situations the severity of stress and it impairing effect on employees should be moderated to the possible extent through the effect of some other variables. The moderators may be antecedent, coexistent or/and subsequent to the incidence of stress. They may be broadly classified as personal and environmental variables. These variables moderate or buffer the severity of stress at three levels, i.e., cognitive (perception and appraisal of stress), response (actual experience of and immediate reactions to stress), and ultimate effect (consequent psychological, behavioural and physical strains). In fact, these variables of positive value add to the coping capability of the focal person and partially compensate to the distress and ultimate strains.

A recent trend of examining the moderating effect of various personal and organizational variables has been initiated by the stress researchers. In increasing number of empirical investigations, researchers have tested the buffering effect of the personal and environmental variables on the relationships of job stress and consequent strains. However, the effect of these variables on the perception or experience of stress has not been extensively investigated. Researchers in India and abroad have examined the moderating effect of several personality and environmental variables on the relationship of occupational stress to consequent strains. Most of the studies revealed that these variables noticeably attenuate the adverse effects of experienced stress on the behaviour and psychological well-being of the focal person. The psychological moderators of stress, strain, and relationship of the two identified by the researchers are reviewed in Table 7.1.

Table 7.1
Psychological Moderators of Stress-Strain Relationship

Psychological Variables	*Investigators*
Type 'A' behaviour pattern	Pestonjee & Singh, 1988
High need for achievement	Srivastava, 1985; Morris & Snyderman, 1979
High need for self-actualization	Srivastava, 1987
Internal locus of control	Beehr et al., 1976; Lefcourt, 1976; Morris & Snyderman, 1979; Pestonjee & Singh, 1981; Srivastava & Krishna, 1992
Sound mental health	Srivastava & Jagdish, 1983
'Approach' mode of coping	Srivastava & Singh, 1987; Srivastava, 1991
Effort and outcome orientation	Pandey & Naidu, 1986
Trust in others	Tiwari, 1986
Cognitive control	Dohrenwend & Dohrenwend, over stressor 1974; Rabkin & Struening, 1976
Self esteem	London & Klimoski, 1975
Flexibility	Kahn, 1973
Higher order needs	Beehr et al., 1976
Effectiveness of defences	Cobb, 1974
Resistance to resources	Antonovsky, 1974
Capacity for wakefulness	Ostberg, 1973
Work values	Crain, 1974

Stress researchers (Kahn and Quinn, 1970; Lazarus and Cohen; 1976) identified a number of individual characteristics which mediate both cognitive appraisal process and coping behaviour. These mediators which buffer the severity of perceived stress are the following:

1. Individual's behavioural skill repertoire (assertiveness, problem solving, conflict resolution);
2. Onc's past cxperience with similar stress;
3. Individual's sound physical and mental state;
4. Availability and quality of one's social support both at work and outside work;
5. Personality factors (self-esteem, Type-A, flexibility-rigidity);
6. Advance working one has of an approaching stressful event;
7. Low intensity and frequency of other chronic and/or discrete stressful events;
8. Low or no constraints of social, cultural or organizational norms;
9. Availability and quality of organizational processes and programmes which aid or facilitate an individual's coping efforts (training); and
10. The extent individual feels freedom and autonomy.

The organizational and social variables which have been noted by the stress researchers to moderate the relationship between job stress and various parameters of strain are enlisted in Table 7.2.

Table 7.2
Organizational and Social Moderators of Stress-Strain Relationship

Organizational/ Social Variables	*Investigators*
Congenial and motivating organizational climate	Singh, 1988; James & Jones, 1974
Positive job attitudes	Srivastava & Jagdish, 1989
Job involvement	Innes & Addreinne, 1985; Srivastava, 1990

Social support	Pinneau, 1976; Cobb, 1976; House & Wells, 1977; LaRacoo & Jones, 1978
Supportive colleagues/ boss	Caplan, 1971; Gore, 1973, 1978; LaRacoo & Jones, 1978
Leadership style (considerate, consistent, employee-oriented and supportive)	Fleishman, Harris, & Burtt, 1955; Fieldler, 1967
Job enrichment	Abel-Halim, 1974
Autonomy on job	Beehr, 1976
Organizational structure	James & Jones. 1976
Flat organization	Ivancevich & Donnelly, 1975.
Opportunity for formal control	Gemmill & Heisler, 1972
Group cohesiveness	Beehr et al., 1976
Interpersonal ties and involvement	Antonovski, 1974
Community involvement	Antonovski, 1974

Besides the above-mentioned variables, several other personal (such as, self-confidence, optimism, high ego-strength, sociability, job experience and competence, high tolerance, etc.) and organizational (such as, high or extra rewards or returns, high job level, group cohesiveness and high industrial morale, participative management, etc.) are also quite likely to alleviate the impairing effects of experienced job stress. The negative or undesirable feeling aroused by the stressors are buffered or compensated by the effect of positive feeling generated by the moderator-variables. Further, the intervention of the moderators attenuates the effectivity of stress in causing different sorts of strain. Management and the employees in the organizations should make all possible efforts to develop, introduce, and enhance the level of above-mentioned buffers in order to attenuate the severity of experienced organizational stresses as well as its undesirable outcomes.

Social Support as Stress Buffer

It would be regarded by most people as mere common sense of claim that, people cope better with stresses if they are well supported by the people around them. Particularly in India, social relations and support have been a great source of relief from stresses of life since the origin of structured society and social groups. It has been an integral feature of our social life. Even in present times, in our day-to-day life we expect and most of the times receive too the help or social support even from those whom we do not personally know. The sense of social support provides us a feeling of security and psychological energy to deal with stress and face undesirable consequences. Low level of stress and anxiety among people in India in general may be attributed, to a large extent, to their sense of high social support. Although role of social support in alleviating psycho-social stress was recognized by social scientists long back, empirical studies of social support in organizations are a recent phenomenon.

Social support can be referred to as people's perception of their social network as containing individuals in whom they can confide, on whom to rely and from whom they expect help, if needed. In most of the studies, social support has been measured by asking subjects to rate how much they could rely on people to get help from them, or to be listened by them. Three groups of people were considered: the supervisors, other people at work, friends and relatives. Perceived participation in decision making was also taken as a measure of social support. The studies revealed that perceived social support alleviated perceived stressors (such as responsibility for persons, role ambiguity and underutilization of skills and abilities). Social support also reduced the consequent strains, such as dissatisfaction, depression and anxiety (Caplan, et al., 1975; Cobb, 1976). Besides the direct effect of social support in alleviating the severity of perceived stress and strains, its buffering effect on the relationship between perceived stress and consequent strain has also been established in some studies (Caplan, 1971; Gore, 1973). It has also been observed that low sense of social support itself is a source of stress. Pinneau (1975) has suggested that process of social support or informal and congenial relationships has three potential effects: (1) directly on the source of stress (preventive); (2) directly on strains or well-being (therapeutic); and (3) moderating effect on stress-strain relationship (buffering).

Mechanism of Social Support

According to Lieberman (1982) social support and resources can influence both the occurrence and the effect of stress in a variety of ways:

(1) Social support can decrease the likelihood of the occurrence of stressful events.
(2) If the event occurs, interaction with significant others can modify or alter the individual's perception of the particular event and hence mitigate the stress potential.
(3) Stress levels are partially contingent on the degree to which a potentially stressful event alters role functioning. Social resources can alter the relationship between role strain and the stress inducing events.
(4) Social resources can influence coping strategies and in this way modify the linkage between stress event and its effect.
(5) To the degree that stressful events erode self-esteem and feelings of personal mastery, social support can modify such effects.
(6) There may be a direct influence of social support and social resources on adaptation level.

The above discussion makes it apparent that social support is an easy and effective remedy of stress. Employees may be suggested to improve their interpersonal competence and to develop dependable relationships on—as well as off the—job at individual level in order to moderate the severity of stress and consequent strains of their job life. At organization level, management should make efforts to create a climate of congenial relationships, intra-cadre and inter-cadre support and co-operation and mutual trust in the organization in order to moderate the severity of occupational stress and strains, and also to buffer the relationship between occupational stress and consequent job and health strains.

Job Involvement as Moderator of Stress-Strain Relationship.

Employees' job involvement has been noted as a predominant factor influencing their job attitudes and job behaviour. It has also been empirically established that employees involved in their job experience lesser job stress. Job involvement also buffers the relationship of occupational stress and consequent job and health related strains. In an extensive study, the author (1990), examined the moderating effect of job involvement on the relationship of occupational stress and mental ill-health in two samples of the employees operating in public and private sector organizations. The obtained data were analyzed in terms of Moderated Multiple Regression in order to examine the moderating effect of job involvement on the relationship of job stress and mental health of the employees. Firstly, the scores on the measure of mental ill-health were regressed on occupational stress and job involvement scores to find out linear multiple correlation (RI). Further, the interaction equation, i.e., product of occupational stress and job involvement, was added to the basic equation, and mental health scores were again regressed on it. Thus, the three variable approach had been used to find out the moderated multiple correlation (RM). Finally, difference between RI and RM was tested by computing F-value. The obtained results are recorded in following Tables (7.3 and 7.4).

Table 7.3
Moderated Multiple Regression Analysis for Job Involvment of the Public Sector Employees (N=450)

Independent Moderating Variables	*Mental Ill-Health* *Ry*	*Ry^2*	*df*	*F*
Occupational Stress (O.S.)	.422 (r)	.177	1,448	96.35*
Occupational Stress (OS), Job Involvement (J.I.)	.438 (RI)	.192	2,447	08.32*
O.S., J.I., O.S. x J.I.	.448 (Rm)	.021	3,446	05.02*

The results (Table 7.3) indicate that job involvement of the public sector employees significantly moderated the relationship of their perceived occupational stress and mental ill-health. The addition of the product of occupational stress and job involvement to the basic equation of occupational stress and job involvement led to a noticeable increase in the variance of mental ill-health of these employees. Though the multiple regression analysis does not specify the direction of the interaction effect of employees' job involvement, the observed inverse relationship between job involvement and occupational stress enable us to conclude that job involvement buffers the degree of positive relationship between occupational stress and mental ill-health of the public sector employees.

Table 7.4
Results of the Moderated Multiple Regression Analysis for Job Involvement of the Private Sector Employees (N=450)

Indian and Modern Variables	*Mental Ill-Health* Ry	Ry^2	*Df*	*F*
Occupl. Stress (O.S)	.137 (r)	.0187	1,448	8.55*
O.S., Job Involv. (J.I.)	.140 (RI)	.0196	2,447	0.41 (N.S)
O.S., J.I., O.S. x J.I.	.141(Rm)	.0198	3,446	0.09 (N.S.)

* = P< .01

r = Zero order correlation

RI = Linear multiple correlation

Rm= Moderated multiple correlation

The results (Table 7.4) make it apparent that job involvement of the employees in private sector organizations did not extend any noticeable moderating effect on the relation of their job stress and mental health. Job involvement of these employees remained ineffective in moderating the adverse effect of occupational stress on mental ill-health of these employees.

In explanation of the observed moderating effect of job involvement on the relationship of occupational stress and mental ill-health of the employees in public sector organizations, it may be argued that the employees committed to and involved in their jobs, consider the job stress as an inevitable part of their jobs, and perceive the challenges and hardships of their jobs as opportunities to satisfy their needs for achievement and personal growth. Such attitudes and tendencies of the involved employees buffer the impairing effects of the inconveniences and constraints of job life on their psychological well being.

Job efficiency and high self-esteem associated with high job involvement, make the employees confident of their calibre to effectively cope with stressful job situations. The 'approach' coping strategies, generally adopted by the job involved employees to deal with their job stresses, itself is a symptom of sound mental health. Srivastava and Singh (1988) have accordingly noted in their study that approach mode of coping moderates the intensity of inverse relationships between organizational role stress and mental health. Besides, the employees considerably involved in their job psychologically identify with their work and consider it as a "central life interest", therefore, their satisfactory adjustment at work is very likely to make them satisfied with and well adjusted to other life domains, which ultimately facilitate improving their overall psychological health. The results of the present study are in conformity with the findings of the previous researches in this regard. Innes and Addreinne (1985) concluded that relationship between life stress and psychological symptoms of illness are moderated by the extent to which a person is involved in his/her job.

Personality Traits and Attributions as Moderator

Personality characteristics of the employees are important mediators of their stress as well as consequent strains. These personality attributes, such as self-esteem, flexibility, locus of control, resistance have also been noted to markedly moderate the relationship between occupational stress and consequent job and health strains. In a recent study on a sample of industrial workers, Srivastava and Veena (1999) noted that personality traits of emotional stability, independence, and practicality, buffered the inverse relationship between occupational stress and job satisfaction, and the positive relationship between occupational stress and psychomatic symptoms.

Locus of control of the employees also has been found to influence their perception of stressors and reactions to felt stress. In several studies, internal locus of control has been found to be associated with low job stress. Since the employees with internal locus of control perceive the situations of stress as a resultant of their own actions and decisions, they perceive to have more control over them. This sense of control moderates the severity of stress and consequent strains. It has been suggested by some researchers that locus of control may be used as moderator, affording some predictions of how an individual copes with stress (Sandler, et al., 1983; Lefcourt, 1983).

Employees attributions for their success and failure on the job have also been reported to moderate the relationship of occupational stress and consequent strains. In a recent study, Gupta (1999) noted that employees' high attribution to effort, work conditions, nature of work, and managerial policy, for their performance on the job, intensified the positive relationship of role stress and health strains, whereas the relationship between the two was alleviated in case of those who highly attributed chance or luck for their success or failure on the job.

8
THERAPEUTIC TREATMENT OF STRESS-DISORDERS

Despite all possible efforts to prevent and mitigate the stress, existence of certain types of occupational stress and its adverse effects cannot be totally controlled or eliminated. These inevitable and consistent stresses, and some severe stresses of job life, result in various types of physical and psychological pathologies among some of the employees possessing certain personality characteristics vulnerable to stress-disorders. At this stage, the affected employees need suitable therapeutic treatment. A number of techniques have been developed and are being used for the treatment of stress-disorders. Progressive relaxation, yoga, meditation, hypno-suggestion, biofeedback, autogenic training, cognitive therapy; music therapy, etc., are the popular techniques for management of stress and treatment of severe strains. Yoga, meditation, and autogenic training are useful in prevention of stress as well as treatment of severe strains. Since most of these techniques have already been discussed as preventive intervention strategies, only remaining techniques have been discussed in brief in this section.

Hypnosuggestive Therapy

In most of the present day therapies hypnosuggestions are used as a part. The suggestions are used alone, as one component of an eclectic approach that integrates procedures from various other techniques such as behavioural, cognitive, rational-emotive, and psychologically oriented therapies. The many different types of suggestions that are submitted under the broader term "hypnosuggestions" derive from the very long historical tradition of suggestive therapeutics and hypnosis. The emphasis in hypnosuggestive technique is on deliberate use by the therapists of suggestions that are intended to help the client in coping with stress and with general and particular difficulties of life. Within a mutually trusting and congruent relationship, the hypnosuggestive therapist aims to present useful suggestions that are specific for each client. The suggestions given specially to the patients of stress-disorders aims to produce deep relaxation, calmness, "letting go", and "awayness" from daily concerns.

After receiving the suggestion, the subject typically show reductions in respiratory rate, skin conductance, and other psychophysiological indices of arousal, and they report that they are relaxed in body and mind (Edmonston, 1981). Barber (1993) has noted that deep relaxation suggestions are used in most of the hypnosuggestive therapies with following reasons:

(1) To define the situation to the subject as hypnosis, because hypnosis leads him to believe that hypnosis is a uniquely powerful tool,
(2) They are easy suggestions that most of the subjects pass, and they thus provide the subjects with the experience of successfully responding to suggestions,
(3) They help in enhancing responsiveness by reducing critical and analytical thinking,
(4) They can change the situation so that imagining and fantasizing are appropriate,
(5) They can produce peace of mind and calmness, which are useful in:

    (a) thinking through solutions to life problems,
    (b) mentally practicing carrying out particular task such as being at ease and calm,
    (c) mentally rehearsing overcoming additions (such

as smoking or alcoholism),

(6) Suggestions for deep relaxation can help in producing a longer-lasting peace of mind and calmness, which are useful for overcoming stress-related disorders such as migraines, headaches, asthma, insomnia, and hypertension.

Philosophical Hypnosis

Barber (1993) has proposed "philosophy of living" to place the active relaxation in the broader context. He suggests the clients to accept this philosophy which is based on four tenets. These tenets are directly implemented and practiced in the hypnotic situation. The major tenets of this philosophical approach for coping with the difficulties of life are as follows:

1. For every human being, life has both desirable and undesirable aspects. Aging, death or many other adverse situations are inevitable for everyone who has come in this world. Also, either we or the people we love will experience, severe pains, birth defects, paralysis, blindness, major physical and mental illness, and many other undesirable happenings. Every human being will also experience other unwanted events. The first and most essential facet of wisdom and ability to live happily is to "fully accept at a deep level that life inevitably has problems, and that virtually every day we will encounter events and behaviours from others that we do not like and that we wish would never occur. These are the parts of our life."

2. The second principle of wisdom is to accept deeply and calmly the immediate difficulty as one of life's undesirable events that happens to face us now, by stating calmly to ourselves, "I have this undesirable happening now in my life. Can I change it for better, and, if so, how?"

3. The third principle of wisdom is to realize deeply that we cannot change things we do not like. We cannot change any event that has already occurred. We cannot change what we have already done, or what has already happened. We can influence only some events that will occur from now, but only to a certain degree. We must try

our best to influence the happenings by changing our attitude and behaviour.

4. The fourth major principle of wisdom is that we can improve our life situations by (a) thinking ahead calmly so that we can encounter people and situations with preparation and serenity; (b) changing ourselves so that we are more accepting, compassionate, and loving toward ourselves and others; (c) emphasizing the positive aspects of and potentials of ourselves and others; (d) modelling for others; (e) when others look up to us and wish to learn from us, talking to them and gently guiding them in an accepting and loving way.

Inhibition-Confrontation Technique

Since early 1900s Pennibaker has been examining the physiological and health consequences of confiding versus not confiding in others about a traumatic event. Inhibited traumatic events or emotions become the focus of obsessive thoughts for several years or decades. Obsessive thinking and the resultant anxiety are associated with increased physiological activity. Fowles (1980) provides evidence indicating that in such a condition, the individual is required to make extra physiological activity to avoid obsessive thinking. Short-term inhibition is reflected in phasic autonomic changes, such as increase in skin conductance, heart rate, and blood pressure. While long-term inhibitions are associated with gross cognitive impairments and stress related diseases. It has also been reported that the individual actively avoiding confronting traumatic emotions, experience trauma-relevant feelings associated with negative-affective areas in the right cortical hemisphere (Davidson, 1980). On contrary to inhibition, consciously confronting the feeling associated with a traumatic event allows for the integration or cognitive restructuring of the events. The confronting act then allows the individual to forget or to put the event behind them, thus reducing physiological activity by negating the need for further obsessing and inhibiting. Confiding in others or freely writing about the stressful experiences often allows for social comparisons, feedback, coping information, and various forms of positive reinforcement (Lazarus & Folkman, 1984). It also helps the person to organize cognitively or work through, reframe, and find meaning to the experience. These cognitive effects help the individual in putting the trauma behind him. Studies suggest that talking or writing about major upheavals may ultimately reduce health problem as well as unwanted thoughts about the events. In addition, the act of talking about a personal trauma makes the individual feel closer to one who is being confided to, thus increasing the power of social support. Jourard (1971), a pioneer of self-disclosure research, noted that talking with others or even writing about ones problem could ultimately reduce or prevent health problems.

In explanation of why self-expression of the frustrating events or experiences therapists have argued that talking with others about traumatic experiences helps in bringing about a new understanding of the experience. Cognitive therapists suggest that by talking or writing about an event, the individual reframes it, which results in a deeper understanding of it. On similar lines, some social psychologists have stressed the importance of finding meaning to an event. These researches have impirically verified that individuals who find meaning in tragic events cope much better than those who do not find meaning. The primary value of reframing or finding meaning in a trauma is that it helps the individual to organize and assimilate the experience. The act of talking or writing about overwhelming traumas helps to bring about assimilation because it gradually levels and sharpens different parts of the experience. As portions are understood, they became assimilated. This process may continue until the entire experience is assimilated and cognitively 'filed away'. Besides, repeated writing or talking about the trauma helps bring about the habituation of the emotional response to the event. Further, expression of the feelings forces the individual publicly to acknowledge its existence and impact.

Recently an extensive study was conducted by Yadav and Srivastava (1996) to examine the effectiveness of confrontational writing in alleviating job stress and consequent job and health strains in a sample of industrial workers. The intervention programme was conducted on the workers selected on the criteria of low self-disclosure.

tendency and high occupational stress. The programme required the selected employees to freely write for fifteen minutes (twice a week) about the strenuous events they confronted with and their feelings and reactions (expressed or unexpressed) to these events or situations. The intervention programme continued for 20 weeks. The results indicated that there was significant decline in a subject's occupational stress and rate of absenteeism, enhancement in their job satisfaction, and improvement in their physical and psychological health as the result of the confrontational writing intervention.

Self-Talk Therapy of Stress and Anxiety

The self-talk therapy proposed by Girodo (1977) is based on cognitive restructuring. A recent and popular trend in behaviour therapy centres on cognitive factors that mediate behaviour change. It focuses on client's perceptions, attributions, and self-evaluations, or the kinds of statements the client makes to himself in appraising the significance of his behaviour. Semantic therapists such as Frank (1961) and Beck (1970) considered maladaptive behaviour and emotional upset as a result of faulty belief systems and faulty cognitive patterns. In this therapy focus was on influencing the irrational premises and assumptions that underlie the client's images, cognitive and self-evaluations. Arbitrary inferences, magnification and over generalizations regarding situations and behaviour leads to faulty evaluations and result in stress and anxiety. Beck (1970) tried to change the client's thinking style in the hope of inducing less anxiety-provoking resolutions of stressful situations. Meichenbaum (1975) attempted to convince the client to self-instruct himself and to emit self-statements that could serve to guide new thoughts or prompt coping behaviour. Self-instructional training in the form of emitting positive self-statements play an effective functional role in interrupting ongoing automatic behavioural or emotional events. These positive self-statements often serve more as attention diversion devices, and this process reduces anxiety or changes cognitive and behaviour patterns.

People talk to themselves while anticipating or preparing for a particular interaction at various points throughout a sequence of behavioural responses, and follow the execution of these responses when evaluating the significance of the interactions. Positive, optimistic and logical self-talking brings desirable change in individual's beliefs and attitudes, and so in the appraisals about the situation, others and ownself. These changes ultimately reduce the severity of stress and reactions to it. In explanations for why self-talk leads to change in cognitive evaluations and behaviour patterns, it may be extended that, there are three different but interdependent psychological processes which operate when people are induced to making positive and coping self-statements in a stressful situation. Girodo (1977) has classified the explanations to efficacy of self-instructional training in reducing stress and anxiety under three headings: (i) self-persuasion, (ii) attention-diversion, and (iii) cognitively cued behaviour.

Self-persuasion: The process of self-persuasion centers on a statement about the functional relation between events and is generally expressed in terms of a belief concerning the causal relations among these events. Clients are persuaded through rational means, that the manner in which they previously evaluated the significance of a particular situation or other's behaviour, is erroneous, and that the new thinking styles and bases for inferences and attributions should be used. In these cognitive restructuring attempts, the concerned person must be induced to accept new thinking and bases, and only then he would convince and persuade himself into a new conceptual organization concerning how events are now to be interpreted and appraised. On this basis, a natural change in self-talking would follow.

Attention diversion: Self-talking can also divert one's attention which would prevent him from (i) focusing upon external stimuli that could lead to anxiety responses or (ii) making negative and self-defeating evaluations which in themselves could cause anxiety. Attention-diversion strategy has been effectively used in the studies dealing with coping with pain. In these studies, subjects were induced to attend to a variety of images and thoughts, or to the task of generating covert or overt verbal statements. The statements were found to be effective in diverting subjects' attention from the pain and in reducing subjective intensity of pain. But these attempts to persuade people to divert attention through self-statements for controlling stress of any nature may have only short lived effects.

***Cognitively Cued Behaviour*:** This behaviour is the process involved in the method in which self-instructional statements can direct to other talk, inferences and attributions. The self-instructional talk designed to cue behaviour and thoughts would prove useful mechanism which attempts to promote behaviour change and acquisition of new behaviour. It is assumed here that self-verbalization of failure and inadequacy increases anxiety when a person appraises the significance of failure. People who practice a self-instructional approach in handling a stressful situation would perform better and experience decreased anxiety. These positive outcomes may be attributed to the operation of mechanisms of attention-diversion and cognitively cued behaviour.

Stress Management Through Music Therapy

Maranto (1993) has extensively discussed the use of music in the management of stress and strains. Music is integral to our daily life. Apart from its aesthetic and entertainment values, there are repeated and consistent descriptions of its uses. The close association between music and medicine can be traced to ancient cultures, where music was closely allied with medical practice. Out of the interest in examining its uses to promote human health and well-being has grown the discipline of music therapy. Its most important therapeutic aspects is its use to facilitate relaxation. Empirical studies on psychological and physiological responses to music started by the end of the nineteenth century. These studies noted the effect of music on neurosis (Corning, 1899), insomnia and fevers (Devison, 1899), and blood pressure, circulation, cardiac contraction, and respiration. Other early researchers concluded that physiological functions responded reflexively to music, and that the subject's appreciation for the music was the important determinant of physiological response (Vincent & Thompson, 1929). These ideas established the foundation for using music to improve health, and supported a rationale for its use in stress management. However, because of the complexity of musical stimuli and the individual differences in responses to music, it is not always easy to generalize the effects of music on health and its effectiveness in stress management. Moreover, responses to music are multidimensional, which occurs at physiological, psychological and cognitive levels simultaneously. Thaut (1989a) concluded that physiological responses to music are the product of individual's unique physiological and psychological makeup, which is further influenced by individualized psychological experience of music.

Physiological Response to Music

It appears that music elicits physiological responses. However, it is not always possible to predict the direction of physiological responses to music, because of the complexity of the musical stimuli and individual differences in responses to music. In a number of studies a variety of physiological responses to music have been observed. Hodges (1980) and Maranto (1993) have summarized the various physiological responses to music after reviewing the researches on effects of music:

Music and Heart Rate

1. Stimulative music increases heart rate; sedative decreases heart rate.
2. Any type of music increases heart rate.
3. Both sedative and stimulative music cause changes in heart rate; however, the directions of these effects are not predictable.
4. Listening to music or toning reduces heart rate.

Elements of Music and Heart Rate

1. Heart rate acceleration is correlated with loudness, tempo, and musical complexity; heart rate deceleration is correlated with resolutions of musical conflict, decreasing loudness, and slowing tempo.
2. Heart rate decelerates to rock music.

Blood Pressure

1. Blood pressure is affected by listening to music, but the type of music that effects these changes is unknown.
2. Music is effective in reducing blood pressure in essential hypertensive.

Respiration

1. Stimulative music increases respiration and sedative music decreases it.
2. Any music increases respiration.
3. Music that is employed increases respiration.
4. Sedative music decreases minute ventilation, minute oxygen usage, and metabolic rate; stimulative music increases these measures slightly.

Digestional Gastric Motality

1. Disliking of the music causes a cessation of gastric motility; sedative music produces stronger stomach contractions.
2. Music decreases stomach acid production.

Muscle Responses

1. Stimulative music increases muscular activity.
2. Listening to music reduces electromyographic (EMG) activity.

Immune Responses

1. Music significantly increases secretery immunoglobulin A (lgA).
2. Entertainment music significantly increases leukocyte circulation.

Psychological Response to Music

Most of the researches on effective responses to music have been concerned with its influence on individual's mood. The results of these researches are summarized below:

(1) Music training influence mood intensity and mood responses elicited by music.

(2) Existing mood of the listener affects subsequent reactions to music. Preference for the music may interact with mood in terms of music's potential to alter mood.

(3) Music is matched to the existing emotional state of the individual and subsequent changes in the mood of the individual.

(4) Psychiatric patients responded appropriately to the moods suggested by words and music. These patients responded more often and consistently than did non-patients.

(5) Significant positive mood changes in cancer patients exposed to live music.

Rationale for the Use of Music Therapy

The following theoretical concepts derived from research findings, reviewed by Maranto (1993), provide support and rationale for the use of music in the management of stress:

1. Music elicits physiological responses, however, the direction of these responses is difficult to predict in a consistent manner.
2. Music elicits psychological (mood/affective) response.
3. Music elicits cognitive responses.
4. Music has the potential for physiological and/or psychological entertainment.
5. Physiological, psychological, and cognitive responses to music are unique for each individual.
6. Music can elicit psychological, cognitive, and physiological responses simultaneously; these responses may be interrelated.
7. Elements of music, as well as the music *gestalt*'s, affect psychological and physiological responses.
8. Vibrational aspects of music may be powerful factors in stress management.
9. Music, because it is predominantly a right-hemisphere function, may be used to block left-hemispheric activity and/or enhance right-hemispheric process.
10. Music can be a reinforcing stimulus for desired

behaviours; music listening or participation is a pleasurable experience.

11. Music can serve as an eliciting stimulus for perceived states of relaxation and positive affective response.
12. Music may serve as a "conditioned stimulus for both sympathetic and parasympathetic autonomic activity".

In stress-literature a number of uses of music have been described. Studies have dealt with the effect of music on anxiety, and management of stress in different anxiety-provoking clinical situations. Music was found to be effective in decreasing physiological tension and anxiety. Music was also found to enhance the recovery from stressful situation (Little, 1986). Music used for relaxation may influence the potential for anxiety reduction. Effect of music in reducing stress and anxiety associated with music performance (Maranto, 1989, 1992). Music therapy techniques significantly reduced anxiety, increased confidence, and decreased narcissism in musicians. Music has also been found effective in reducing stress among the gynaecological patient undergoing punch biopsy (Davis, 1991); among children undergoing bone marrow transplants and lumber puncutes (Schur, 1986); and patients undergoing bronchoscopy procedures (Metzler & Berman, 1991). Music has also been found improving mood and comfort of adult patients in general hospital and intensive care units, and it has also been found reducing stress hormone level during surgery.

However, the effect of music in reducing or moderating job stress and consequent strains has not been extensively examined. Since it is an easy intervention, it should be used in industries for improving work environment and reducing stresses prevailing in workplace.

9

SOME RELATED ISSUES AND SUGGESTIONS

Although all the stress management techniques discussed earlier purport to get employees relief from stresses of job life, each has its own specific modality and orientation as well as specific utility. Thus, selection of a suitable intervention technique for preventing or mitigating the stressors or for moderating or treating the strains of specific types for a particular employee or a group of employees seems to be a crucial decision. The stress management practitioner should take into consideration the 'specificity' of the intervention techniques, as well as individual differences in response to a particular intervention strategy while selecting the stress management technique and assessing its effects.

Specificity of Stress Management Techniques

Various stress management techniques obviously differ in their primary objectives, modalities, and specific effects. Some of the interventions primarily prevent the stress-situations, some of them moderate or mitigate the stress, and some of them purport to moderate or cure specific psychological or somatic symptoms of different severity. It has also been observed that these strategies or techniques also differin their effectivity in reducing stress and consequent strains. The specific effect hypothesis was formulated by Davidson and Schwarty (1976) who cited the findings of desynchronies among cognitive, behavioural, and somatic measures of anxiety. The hypothesis suggests that a treatment oriented to one of these modalities would particularly benefit the symptoms of that modality: cognitive treatment for cognitive symptoms, behavioural treatment for behavioural symptoms and somatic treatment for somatic symptoms. For example, progressive relaxation and biofeedback are primarily somatically oriented, and cognitive techniques have cognitive orientation. Autogenic training has both cognitive and somatic aspects and has a greater emphasis on autonomic effects. Mantra meditation was first categorized as a somatic technique, but later it was reclassified as a cognitive technique because saying a verbal mantra might be expected to block verbal anxiety-related thoughts directly (Schwartz, Davidson, Goleman, 1978). This indicates that various stress management techniques have highly specific effects, as well as more generally stress-reducing effects.

However, in some studies no differences could be found among the effects of various contrasting stress-reduction techniques. In most of these studies, the methods themselves contained elements of more than one treatment modality. I am also of the opinion that ultimate effect of all the techniques is reduction in stress, though it comes through different channels (i.e., cognitive, behavioural, or somatic). These components of human-system cannot be separated. Although the emphasis of a technique may be on either of these three components, but it affects the whole system. For example, the emphasis of cognitive therapy is on cognitive restructuring through a change in cognitive components. But it can effectively reduce the psychological as well as somatic symptoms of stress. Similarly, the learning of some new specific behaviour patterns can modify the cognitive patterns.

Individual Differences in Response to Stress Intervention Technique

Similar to the differential effects of various stress management techniques, the individuals also differ in their responses to various techniques of distress reduction. Individuals' personality characteristics are one of the major source of difference in this regard. Besides the personality traits, individuals' expectancy for success, locus of control, depression, psychophysiological reactivity, hypnotic susceptibility, beliefs, attitudes and values play important role in determining their responses to the treatments given for stress management.

Expectancy for success is an important ingredient in the success of any psychological treatment. Difference in individuals' expectancy for success of the treatment cause significant variance in responses to the treatment. Brown (1977) found that positive expectancy was important in treating with relaxation therapy. Willingness to practice and a belief that the method is effective and useful enhances the effect of the treatment.

The effect of expectancy interact with internal locus of control in making the therapy more effective with internally oriented clients. Subjects who believe that they can exercise personal control over events might therefore be expected to practice any stress-reduction technique more than the subjects who believe that events are controlled by external forces. Lewis, Biglan, and Steinbock (1978) found that the subject with internal locus of control also had high expectancy for success and practiced the exercise more at home. They, consequently showed greater reduction in stress and anxiety than others. Locus of control also independently associates with willingness to engage in various self-management strategies. Dinning and Crampton (1989) found that locus of control to be positively associated with engaging in preventive health behaviours. There is evidence that internal locus of control may be a positive predictor of success in programmes, which include biofeedback, relaxation training, and cognitive interventions. The positive relationship between internal locus of control and success of the interventions may reflect a greater willingness on the part of internally oriented subjects to practice and apply the technique, perhaps turning from their assumption that they can in fact exercise control over their stress levels.

Another factor which cause variance in an individuals' response to stress management interventions is depression. It has been established by stress management practitioners that depressed persons are often not helped by the stress management techniques. Subjects with lower level of maladjustment tend to enjoy and practice meditation more than others. Level of physiological arousal or reactivity also affects responses to various stress-reduction treatments. A positive association has been observed between initial resting heart rate and subsequent response to various behavioural treatments of stress and anxiety. Subjects' hypnotic suggestibility also is an important factor in determining their responses to stress management intervention. Although response to various stress-reducing techniques tend to be related to hypnotic susceptibility, specifically hypnotic techniques tend to show somewhat higher relationship. This probability results from greater similarity of hypnotic procedures to those used in tests of hypnotic susceptibility. Spanos, Ollerhead, and Gwyann (1986) noted the association between hypnotic susceptibility and reduction of induced pain among the subjects with hypnosis, but not with stress inoculation training; however, both techniques lowered the pain reactivity. It has been noted that progressive relaxation technique is more effective than hypnosis for low-hypnotizable subjects, whereas highly hypnotizable show greater responses on most of the measures in both the conditions.

Evaluation of Intervention Programmes

Evaluation of the effectiveness of interventions and modifications for their improvement are also important aspects of stress management. It is also important to ascertain whether there is an adequate 'return' to the organization on the investment it is making in intervention programmes for occupational stress of its employees. Evaluation of the interventions may be also helpful in making necessary modifications for its improvement. Effectiveness of various stress management interventions may be assessed at two levels, i.e., individual level and organizational level. At individual level employees' job stress, physical and psychological health, and coping efficiency must be assessed after the intervention in order to determine the effect of the intervention. Organizational level decrease in employees' absenteeism and turnover, increase in their job satisfaction and performance, and improvement in organizational climate and overall effectiveness may be the criteria for determining positive effects of the given intervention. Standardized measures of the status of general health, occupational stress, role stress, personal strains, burnout, coping resources and strategies, job satisfaction, morale and perceived organizational climate may be employed for the purpose of objectively estimating effectiveness of the intervention techniques. The practitioner should incorporate multiple of the interventions.

Some Guidelines for Application of Interventions

Though a variety of interventions have been suggested by psychologists for management of occupational stress, the ideal study of organizational stress management interventions has yet to be designed. Ivancevich and Matteson (1987) have suggested that if the management of job related stress is to advance, researchers need to adhere to a more systematic programme of applied research. The following questions must be taken into consideration while evolving an effective stress management intervention:

1. What are the relevant factors within the work environment which are potentially stressful?
2. Why do job stressors affect some employees negatively and not the others?
3. What are the consequences of prolonged and unmanaged stress?
4. What type of diagnosis would be the best starting-point for the intervention?
5. What kind of organizational interventions would be the most effective?

Sometimes it becomes quite difficult or impossible to execute the intervention programmes in organization setting in prescribed form. Thus, instead of presenting ideal suggestions the practitioner should offer what seems to be reasonable courses to take in investigating organizational level stress management interventions. In this regard Ivancevich and Matteson (1987) have suggested following guidelines:

Needs Diagnosis

The first step in organizational level stress management is to conduct a needs diagnosis which is the prevalence of stress among employees? Do organizational stressors contribute to these stress levels? Which stressors can be efficiently modified to reduce or minimize the stress? The needs diagnosis is intended to verify that a stress problem exists. In a workplace setting, a needs diagnosis could also examine the incidence and distribution of health, family and performance consequences. Is there a particular unit or group in which excessive health, family and performance consequences are occurring? The next phase of a needs diagnosis is to establish corrective managerial action goals. Specific quantifiable outcome and consequence measures of any corrective action should be discussed and established.

Experimental Design to Assess Programmes' Effectiveness

There have been very few reported studies that have evaluated organizational level stress management interventions. The ideal design would be a true experiment. The one true experimental design is the pre-intervention-post intervention group comparison.

R	O_1	X	O_2	Intervention Group
R	O_1		O_2	Control Group.

R = Randomization; O_1 = Observations or measurements;

X = Intervention; O_2 = Observations (post intervention).

The true experimental design can only be used when the target population is much larger than the programme participants. In a small work setting, where intervention and control groups are likely to interact, contamination of effects may result.

When experimental design is impossible, quasi-experimental design may be adopted. When randomising volunteers to intervention and control groups is not possible, it is useful to find a non-randomized comparison group. The non-equivalent control group design is

O_1	x	O_2	Intervention Group
O_1	x	O_2	Control Group

A second quasi-experimental design is the semi series design, which is

O_1 O_2 x O_3 O_4

Longitudinal Research

There is a void in the literature in the development of comprehensive theories of how to manage stress. Longitudinal data can provide necessary empirical base for developing these needed comprehensive theories. Longitudinal research on stress management intervention at organizational level would permit the observation, description, and classification of stressors, stress, outcomes, and consequences in such a way that the stress process can be empirically documented as a dynamic phenomenon. The longitudinal studies of the management of organizational stress requires a longer time-frame than one week, one month, or three months. The time span must be of sufficient length to permit changes in outcomes and consequences to unfold. One year sees to be a reasonable starting-point in tracking whether an organizational level inter-vention is having an impact on outcomes and consequences.

Outcome and Consequence Measures

Improvement of outcome and consequence variables is of great importance in ascertaining effectiveness of organizational level stress management interventions. Research designs and methodologies need to incorporate multiple outcome and consequence measures. For example, if intervention is found to reduce absenteeism but changes in psychophysiological reactivity such as blood pressure or apathy are occurring, then a more comprehensive understanding of intervention mechanism can be achieved. Since the intervention-consequence mechanisms are not fully understood or known, then organizational level intervention research can be conducted as much to develop insights on mechanisms as to identify useful model of intervention.

Methods of Intervention

It is quite crucial to decide whether to adopt a multimodal or single method intervention strategy. Majority of individual level interventions use single method approach, such as relaxation, cognitive restructuring or behavioural changes. Single method is more precise and demands either theoretical or empirical reasons for selecting a specific intervention, but has a risk of lack of results for so many reasons. Research at organizational level should use both approaches for differing insights offered by them. The multimodal method is more likely to provide information on the methodology for promoting improvements, while the single method approach is more likely to test hypothesis about mechanism.

A primary deficiency in individual level intervention research is lack of controls. Control should be incorporated into research designs to the maximum possible extent. However, even when controls cannot be incorporated in the research design it could be important to gather information about how individuals have been affected by their involvement with an organizational level stress management intervention. Even a no control group situation can reveal whether an intervention is having some affect. The researchers must recognize the potential complexity of organizational level interventions. Individual level interventions should not be replaced by organizational level interventions.

It would be better if the stress management interventions designed to be made at individual and organizational levels are combined together. We must keep this fact in our minds that total elimination of stressors by using intervention strategies is beyond the ability of any manager or stress management practitioner. It is also not a healthy practice to keep employees totally free from stress. A moderate level of stress is necessary for generating arousal and motivation among the employees. Management should therefore pay greater attention to organizational factors which might cause stress, such as intrinsic job factors, organizational structure and culture, reward system, human resource systems, and leadership system. This increased attention could result in the improvement in performance, physical and psychological health, and family life of the employees. The employees should be convinced by the practitioner to accept the fact that stress is an inevitable part of our lives, and they can most conveniently manage it at their cognitive and behavioural levels by themselves.

Appendix- I
Occupational Stress Index

A.K. Srivastava & A.P. Singh

The scale assesses the extent of stress, employees experience in context of their job life. Select any one of the five alternative responses to indicate the extent of accuracy to which each statement describes the nature and conditions at your job, and your experiences and feelings about various aspects of your job life.

To estimate the level of your occupational stress add up the scores on all the statements. If the score is below 115, you have low occupational stress, if the score is between 116 and 161, your occupational stress is of moderate level, and if the score is above 161, you are highly stressed. The statements with asterix should be scored inversely, e.g., 5 for absolutely false, and 1 for absolutely true.

Sl. No.	*Statement*	*Absolutely True* 5	*Almost True* 4	*Partially True* 3	*Almost False* 2	*Absolutely False* 1
1	I have to do a lot of work in this job.	( )	( )	( )	( )	( )
2	The available informations relating to my job-role and its outcomes are vague and insufficient.	( )	( )	( )	( )	( )

		5	4	3	2	1
3	My different officers often give contradictory instructions regarding my work.	( )	( )	( )	( )	( )
4	Sometimes it becomes complicated problem for me to make adjustment between political/group pressures and formal rules and instructions.	( )	( )	( )	( )	( )
5	The responsibility for the efficiency and productivity of many employees is thrust upon me.	( )	( )	( )	( )	( )
*6	Most of my suggestions are heeded and implemented here	( )	( )	( )	( )	( )
*7	My decisions and instructions concerning distribution of assignments among employees are properly followed.	( )	( )	( )	( )	( )
8	I have to work with persons of my liking.	( )	( )	( )	( )	( )
9	My assignments are of monotonous nature.	( )	( )	( )	( )	( )
*10	Higher authorities do care for my self-respect.	( )	( )	( )	( )	( )
11	I get less salary in comparison to the quantum of my labour/work.	( )	( )	( )	( )	( )
12	I do my work under tense circumstances.	( )	( )	( )	( )	( )
13	Owing to excessive workload I have to manage with insufficient number of employees and resources.	( )	( )	( )	( )	( )
*14	The objectives of my work-role are quite clear and adequately planned.	( )	( )	( )	( )	( )
*15	Officials do not interfere with my jurisdiction and working methods.	( )	( )	( )	( )	( )

		5	4	3	2	1
16	I have to do some work unwillingly owing to certain group/political pressures.	( )	( )	( )	( )	( )
17	I am responsible for the future of a number of employees.	( )	( )	( )	( )	( )
*18	My co-operation is freuently sought in solving the administrative or industrial problems at higher level.	( )	( )	( )	( )	( )
*19	My suggestions regarding the training-programmes of the employees are given due significance.	( )	( )	( )	( )	( )
20	Some of my colleagues and subordinates try to defame and malign me as unsuccessful.	( )	( )	( )	( )	( )
*21	I get ample opportunity to utilize my abilities and experience independently.	( )	( )	( )	( )	( )
*22	This job has enhanced my social status.	( )	( )	( )	( )	( )
23	I am seldom rewarded for my hard labour and efficient performance.	( )	( )	( )	( )	( )
24	Some of my assignments are quite risky and complicated.	( )	( )	( )	( )	( )
25	I have to dispose off my work hurriedly owing to excessive workload.	( )	( )	( )	( )	( )
26	I am unable to perform my duties smoothly owing to uncertainty and ambiguity of the scope of my jurisdiction and authorities.	( )	( )	( )	( )	( )
27	I am not provided with clear instructions and sufficient facilities regarding the new assignments trusted to me.	( )	( )	( )	( )	( )

		5	4	3	2	1
28	In order to maintain group-conformity sometimes I have to do/produce more than the usual.	( )	( )	( )	( )	( )
29	I bear the great responsibility for the progress and prosperity of this organization.	( )	( )	( )	( )	( )
30	My opinions are sought in framing important policies of the Organization/ Department.	( )	( )	( )	( )	( )
*31	Our interests and opinion are duly considered in making appointments for important posts.	( )	( )	( )	( )	( )
32	My colleagues do cooperate with me voluntarily in solving administrative and industrial problems.	( )	( )	( )	( )	( )
*33	I get ample opportunity to develop my aptitude and proficiency properly.	( )	( )	( )	( )	( )
34	My higher authorities do not give due significance to my position and work.	( )	( )	( )	( )	( )
35	I often feel that this job has made my life cumbersome.	( )	( )	( )	( )	( )
36	Being too busy with official work I am unable to devote sufficient time to my domestic and personal problems.	( )	( )	( )	( )	( )
37	It is unclear what type of work and behaviour my higher authorities and colleagues expect from me.	( )	( )	( )	( )	( )
*38	Employees attach due importance to the official instructions and formal working procedures.	( )	( )	( )	( )	( )

		5	4	3	2	1
39	I am compelled to violate the formal and administrative procedures and policies owing to group/political pressures.	( )	( )	( )	( )	( )
*40	My opinion is sought in changing or modifying the working system, instruments and conditions here.	( )	( )	( )	( )	( )
*41	There exists sufficient mutual cooperation and team-spirit among the employees of this Organization/Department.	( )	( )	( )	( )	( )
42	My suggestions and cooperation are not sought in solving even those problems for which I am quite competent.	( )	( )	( )	( )	( )
*43	Working conditions are satisfactory here from the point of view of our welfare and convenience.	( )	( )	( )	( )	( )
44	I have to do such work as ought to be done by others.	( )	( )	( )	( )	( )
45	It becomes difficult to implement all of a sudden the new dealing procedures and policies in place of those already in practice.	( )	( )	( )	( )	( )
46	I am unable to carry out my assignments to my satisfaction on account of excessive load of work and lack of time.	( )	( )	( )	( )	( )

Appendix II
Functional Job Stress Scale (Short Form)

A.K. Srivastava & A. Krishna

The scale assesses the extent of job stress which is caused from demanding but desirable job situations. Employees react to these situations with positive affect. Choose either of the four alternative responses for each of the statements to indicate the extent to which they are true in your case.

To estimate the level of your functional job stress add up the scores on all the statements. If the score is below 30, your functional stress is low, if score is between 31 and 45, the level of stress is moderate, and if the score is above 45, the stress is of high level.

Sl. No.	*Statement*	*Absolutely True* 5	*Almost True* 4	*Partially True* 3	*Almost False* 2	*Absolutely False* 1
1.	I am delegated some extra responsibilities in addition to my prescribed ones.	( )	( )	( )	( )	( )
2.	I get irritated in explaining to new personnel about their work and respnsibilities.	( )	( )	( )	( )	( )

	5	4	3	2	1
3. I feel that I am not fully capable and competent to bear out my job responsibilities effectively.	( )	( )	( )	( )	( )
4. I have to give extra time due to excessive work load.	( )	( )	( )	( )	( )
5. I am to do some such tasks as ought to be done by others.	( )	( )	( )	( )	( )
6. It becomes very difficult for me to satisfy everyone in distribution of work and responsi- bilities.	( )	( )	( )	( )	( )
7. It becomes difficult and dubious for me to take decision in crucial matters pertaining to subordinates' services.	( )	( )	( )	( )	( )
8. A big burden of supervision and control of a number of employees is on me.	( )	( )	( )	( )	( )
9. I have to be ultimately responsible for the performance of a number of employees.	( )	( )	( )	( )	( )
10. I have been given major responsibility of formulation and/or implementation of important policies.	( )	( )	( )	( )	( )
11. Having excessive job responsibilities, I find it difficult to give sufficient time to my family and friend circle.	( )	( )	( )	( )	( )
12. I have to take crucial decisions in the matters of employees' grievances, transfers and/or promotions.	( )	( )	( )	( )	( )
13. I am given responsibility of solving crucial/emergent problems of the department/ organization.	( )	( )	( )	( )	( )

Appendix III
Stress Symptoms Inventory

The inventory comprises common physical, psychological, and social relational symptoms, which people manifest when they are under stress. Rate these symptoms on 4 point scale to indicate how frequently you experienced these problems (symptoms) in the past one month.

Sl. No.	*Symptoms*	1 *Never*	2 *Sometimes*	3 *Quite Often*	4 *Almost Constantly*
	Physical				
1.	Tension headaches	( )	( )	( )	( )
2.	Fatigue	( )	( )	( )	( )
3.	Weakness	( )	( )	( )	( )
4.	High blood pressure	( )	( )	( )	( )
5.	Hot or cold spells	( )	( )	( )	( )
6.	Heart pounding	( )	( )	( )	( )
7.	Pain in lower part of back	( )	( )	( )	( )
8.	Indigestion	( )	( )	( )	( )
9.	Constipation	( )	( )	( )	( )
10.	Lump in throat	( )	( )	( )	( )
11.	Muscle aches	( )	( )	( )	( )

	1	2	3	4
12. Trembling	( )	( )	( )	( )
13. Upset stomach	( )	( )	( )	( )
14. Gastric trouble	( )	( )	( )	( )
15. Rash	( )	( )	( )	( )
Psychological				
16. Feeling tense	( )	( )	( )	( )
17. Anxiety (Vague fear)	( )	( )	( )	( )
18. Depression	( )	( )	( )	( )
19. Irritability	( )	( )	( )	( )
20. Mood swing	( )	( )	( )	( )
21. Temper outbursts	( )	( )	( )	( )
22. Feeling of hopelessness	( )	( )	( )	( )
23. Low enthusiasms	( )	( )	( )	( )
24. Nervousness	( )	( )	( )	( )
25. Frustration	( )	( )	( )	( )
26. Crying pells	( )	( )	( )	( )
27. Worrying about things	( )	( )	( )	( )
28. Negative self talk	( )	( )	( )	( )
29. Boredom	( )	( )	( )	( )
30. Confusion	( )	( )	( )	( )
31. Forgetfulness	( )	( )	( )	( )
32. Poor Concentration	( )	( )	( )	( )
Social Relational				
33. Feeling of loneliness	( )	( )	( )	( )
34. Hiding	( )	( )	( )	( )
35. Intolerance	( )	( )	( )	( )
36. Distrust	( )	( )	( )	( )
37. Decrease in contacts	( )	( )	( )	( )
38. Resentment	( )	( )	( )	( )
39. Feeling Isolated	( )	( )	( )	( )

Appendix IV

Job Anxiety Scale

(Short Form) A.K. Srivastava

The questionnaire purports to assess the level of anxiety, employees manifest in context of their job life. You are required to respond the statements on Yes/No pattern. Give one (1) score for 'Yes' and zero (0) for 'No'. To assess the level of your job anxiety add up the scores on all the statements. If the score is from 0 to 6, level of job anxiety is low, if it is between 7 and 13, the job anxiety level is moderate, and if the score is 14 or above it indicates a high level of job anxiety.

1. I feel that I am unable to perform my work as efficiently as I can. Yes/No
2. I often get worried what will happen to my family if I am turned out of my job. Yes/No
3. I apprehend that my officers and co-workers criticize me. Yes/No
4. I often get worried that I would come under some catastrophe. Yes/No
5. I am often unable to concentrate on my work. Yes/No
6. My officers and co-workers misunderstand me. Yes/No
7. I often feel that my performance is not objectively appraised and given due significance. Yes/No
8. I often apprehend about my promotion. Yes/No

9. My officers chafe at my work (performance) without reasons. Yes/No
10. I think of changing over to some other job. Yes/No
11. I often feel that I have not selected a suitable job. Yes/No
12. Most of the time I find that there is no person among my colleagues in whom I can confide. Yes/No
13. I am afraid of false allegations. Yes/No
14. I sometimes feel that I am not significantly contributing to society. Yes/No
15. I often get worried about my future career. Yes/No
16. I am very sensitive to my relationships with my colleagues. Yes/No
17. I often feel whether I shall be able to discharge my duties and responsibilities efficiently. Yes/No
18. I observe that my colleagues do not express real happiness on my promotion or success or achievements. Yes/No
19. Whenever my officers or supervisors observe my activities I undergo a state of tension and fear. Yes/No
20. I feel that the services of workers of other companies are more secure than those of the workers of this company. Yes/No

Appendix V
Stress Resistant Cognitive Behavioural Patterns Scale

A.K. Srivastava

The scale assesses extent of those cognitive and behavioural patterns, which prevent or moderate the experience of stress in day-to-day life and reactions to them. Choose one of the five alternative responses to indicate how far these statements resemble your cognitive and behavioural orientations. To estimate your resistance to stress add up the scores on all statements. If the score is below 84, resistance is low, if the score is between 85 and 132, your resistance is moderate, and if the score is above 132 it indicates high resistance to stress.

Sl. No.	*Statement*	*Absolutely True* 5	*Almost True* 4	*Partially True* 3	*Almost False* 2	*Absolutely False* 1
1.	I am confident that I can effectively deal with any difficult situation or problem.	( )	( )	( )	( )	( )
2.	I have optimistic attitude towards life and do not get hopeless in any situation.	( )	( )	( )	( )	( )

	5	4	3	2	1
3. I confine my needs and aspirations within my capability and resources.	( )	( )	( )	( )	( )
4. I perceive difficulties and adversities in broader perspective and react to them positive affect.	( )	( )	( )	( )	( )
5. I accept the realities and bitter truths of life unstrainedly.	( )	( )	( )	( )	( )
6. I ponder clearly and unbiasedly why present difficulty or trouble should not have come.	( )	( )	( )	( )	( )
7. Before taking any decision or making any action, I consider its farreaching outcomes.	( )	( )	( )	( )	( )
8. I keep on thinking about probable difficulties and problems and their solutions.	( )	( )	( )	( )	( )
9. Neither I expect much from others nor do I depend totally on others.	( )	( )	( )	( )	( )
10. Despite best efforts if I get failure, I accept it unstrainedly as God's will.	( )	( )	( )	( )	( )
11. I believe in as well as try to practise the Gita's philosophy that "my right is to work only, but never to the fruit (outcomes) there of".	( )	( )	( )	( )	( )
12. I prioritize my responsibilities or liabilities and take them up accordingly.	( )	( )	( )	( )	( )
13. I am not rigid in my decisions and actions, I modify them according to situation.	( )	( )	( )	( )	( )
14. Despite all efforts if I don't find solution to any problem I leave it to God.	( )	( )	( )	( )	( )
15. I try to find out complete or long term solution to any problem reather than partial or temporary ones.	( )	( )	( )	( )	( )
16. I try to come out of the state of uncertainty or indecisiveness as soon as possible.	( )	( )	( )	( )	( )

	5	4	3	2	1
17. I try to maintain mental poise in situations of both difficulty and happiness or loss and achievement.	( )	( )	( )	( )	( )
18. Usually I do not get over enthusiastic in discharging my duties/ responsibilities.	( )	( )	( )	( )	( )
19. I usually don't commit beyond my capability and resources.	( )	( )	( )	( )	( )
20. Neither I shirk from nor defer my responsibilities.	( )	( )	( )	( )	( )
21. I avoid doing many things simultaneously.	( )	( )	( )	( )	( )
22. I consider the adversities as an inevitable part of life and deal with them patiently.	( )	( )	( )	( )	( )
23. While tackling troublesome situations I Keep in mind its positive or beneficial outcomes.	( )	( )	( )	( )	( )
24. I avoid competing with others, yet I discharge my duties with full competence and sincerity.	( )	( )	( )	( )	( )
25. Though I discharge my duties with full competence and integrity, I don't try for perfection.	( )	( )	( )	( )	( )
26. I try to maintain coordination among family, professional, and social roles.	( )	( )	( )	( )	( )
27. I complete important tasks/ liabilities within due time. I don't defer them for last moment.	( )	( )	( )	( )	( )
28. Usually I don't poke my nose in others' or unnecessary affairs.	( )	( )	( )	( )	( )
29. Despite my busy routine I do spare some time for fun or entertainment.	( )	( )	( )	( )	( )
30. I try to nip in the bud such pretty things that may in due course cause serious problems/troubles.	( )	( )	( )	( )	( )
31. I believe every problem has a solution ultimately.	( )	( )	( )	( )	( )
32. I try to take difficulties and troubles	( )	( )	( )	( )	( )

	Statement	5	4	3	2	1
	as destined and try to deal with them patiently.					
33.	I think there is probably none who is entirely free from worries and troubles.	( )	( )	( )	( )	( )
34.	I believe life is a combination of sorrow and happiness.	( )	( )	( )	( )	( )
35.	I don't compare myself only with those who are better off and more contented, but also with them at times with those who are inferior or less happy and contented.	( )	( )	( )	( )	( )
36.	I believe we can learn something also from adversities or failures	( )	( )	( )	( )	( )

Appendix VI
Coping Strategies Scale

A.K. Srivastava

The scale assesses the extent to which people use various strategies (such as approach, avoidance, cognitive and combination of the preceding three) to deal with the stressful situations in their day-to-day life. Choose any of the five alternative responses for each coping strategy to indicate the frequency of their use in your dealing with the stressful situations.

Since the scale comprises the items on coping strategies of different categories, must be added up separately to assess the extent of use of different modes of coping. However, to assess overall coping, the scores on all the items may be added up.

Sl. No.	*Statement*	*Never* 1	*Rarely* 2	*Sometimes* 3	*Quite Often* 4	*Almost Always* 5
1.	Accept the situation because there is nothing I can do to change it or to get rid of it.					
2.	Devote more time and energy to meet the demands of the situation.					
3.	Discuss with others who could do something concrete about the solution of the problem.					

	1	2	3	4	5
4. Ask people who have had similar experiences. "What did they do"?					
5. Take the situation as an opportunity to learn, and do what is expected of me.					
6. Change my priorities and time-istribution in order to effectively cope with the situation.					
7. Come up with a couple of alternative solutions to the problem.					
8. Bargain or compromise to get something positive from the situation.					
9. Blame myself for the present situation and feel guilty and depressed.					
10. Change to leisure tasks which necessarily bring immediate relief.					
11. Consider the situation as a part of fate or desire of God and try to cope with it patiently.					
12. Instead of misinterpreting or exaggerating the situation, appraise it objectively and take direct action to deal with it.					
13 Consider the stressful situations as inevitable part of life and deal with them in usual manner.					
14. Console myself with the hope that things would be better next time and accept the situation.					
15. Devote more time to prayer and religious thoughts.					
16. Delegate some of the responsibilities to others.					

2 3 4 5

17. Console myself with the thought that the situation is not that bad as it could have been, and deal with positive affect.
18. Try to get sympathy and understanding from others without doing much to deal with the situation.
19. Try to get out of the situation gracefully.
20. React aggressively to those who are responsible for the situation.
21. Keep the aroused feelings confined to myself, and deal with the situation in depressed mood.
22. Leave it for others to decide or resolve the problem.
23. Appraise and deal with the situation with reference to others who are facing with more severe situations.
24. Leave the situation to God to take care of.
25. Try not to make the situation worse by acting so soon, and wait for the right time to do something meaningful.
26. Try for immediate or sooner relief through partial or temporary solutions of the problem.
27. Physically withdraw from the situation temporarily.
28. Postpone taking any decision or action towards solution of the problem.
29. Put aside other activities in order to concentrate on the problem.

	1	2	3	4	5
30. Give extra attention towards planning and scheduling the action, and deal with the situation accordingly.					
31. Deal with the situation patiently with a belief in the philosophy that "my right is to make efforts, not to the fruit thereof."					
32. Leave the situation to take its own course with this belief that passage of time itself is a remedy to many problems.					
33. Request help from the persons who have the authority/resources to do something to help.					
34. Seek company of friends and family leaving the situation aside.					
35. Try to adjust or deal with the situation constrainedly.					
36. Start worrying too much without doing much to solve the problem.					
37. Take situation as a challenge and work harder to deal with it.					
38. Think about unreal things that make me feel me feel better or happy.					
39. Try to release the emotional distress by talking to someone.					
40. Do not take the situation seriously with the attitude that "it is not everything."					
41. Adopt some short-cut or socially disapproved methods to get rid of the situation.					
42. Try to get emotional support from relations and friends in adjusting with the situation.					

	1	2	3	4	5
43. Try to rationalize the situation, and logically think why should it be upsetting and frustrating?					
44. Try to ignore or avoid the situation to the maximum possible extent.					
45. Try for long-term or lasting solutions to the problem even by taking more strain/pain voluntarily.					
46. Do not believe that situation has really taken place.					
47. Take immediate action without thinking much about the ultimate consequences.					
48. Accept the reality and work on changing/modifying the behaviour or policies which caused the situation of stress.					
49. Deal with the situation with positive affect keeping in mind its positive outcomes.					

BIBLIOGRAPHY

- Abel-Halim, & Ahmad, A. (1982). Social support and managerial effective responses to job stress. *Journal of Occupational Behaviour,* 3: 281-95.
- Abel-Halim, A. (1978). Employees effective responses to organizational stress: Moderating effects of job characteristics. *Personnel Psychology,* 31: 561-79.
- Aerospace Medicine Division (1985). G-induced loss of consciousness. USAF: Brooks Air Force Base.
- Agrawal, N.M. (1984). Application of job characteristic approach in management of organizational stress. Comprehensive Examination Paper, O.B. Area, I.I.M., Ahmedabad.
- Agrawal, U.N. (1980). A step to develop a job involvement scale. *Indian Journal of Psychology,* 55: 38-42.
- Akerstedt, T. (1976). *Shift Work and Health*: Interdisciplinary aspects. In P.G. Rentos, & R.D. Shepard (Eds.), *Shift Work and Health.* Washington, D.C.:U.S. Govt. Printing Office.
- Aldwin, C., & Revension, T.A. (1987). Does coping help? A re-examination of the relation between coping and mental health. *Journal of Personality and Social Psychology,* 53: 337-48.
- Allen, R.D., Hitt, M.A., & Greer, C.R. (1982). Occupational stress and perceived organizational effectiveness in formal groups: An examination of stress

level and stress type. *Personnel Psychology*, 35: 359-70.

- Anderson, C.R. (1976). Coping behaviours as intervening mechanisms in the inverted 'U' stress-performance relationship. *Journal of Applied Psychology*, 61: 30-34.
- Antonovsky, A. (1974). Conceptual and methodological problems in the study of resistence, resources and stressful life events. In B.S. Dohrenwood, & B.P. Dohrenwood (Eds.), *Stressful Life Events: Their Nature and Effects*. New York: Wiley.
- Appley, M.H., & Trumbel, R. (1967). *Psychological Stress*. New York: Appleton-Century-Crafts.
- Arthur, H.T., & Gunderson, E.K. (1965). Promotion and mental illness in the Navy. *Journal of Occupational Medicine*, 7: 452-46.
- Baddeley, A.D. (1972). Selective attention and performance in dangerous environment. *British Journal of Psychology*, 72: 537-46.
- Banerjee, R. (1989). Role stress, organizational effectiveness and mental health of the employees of manufacturing & non-manufacturing organizations. Unpublished doctoral dissertation, Banaras Hindu University, Varanasi.
- Barker, T.X. (1993). Hypno-suggestive approaches to stress reduction: Data, theory and applications. In P.M. Leherer & R.L. Woolfolk (Eds.), *Principles and Practice of Stress Management*. The Guilford Press: New York.
- Basowitz, H., Persky, H., Korchin, S.J., & Grinker, R.R. (1958). Anxiety in a life stress. *Journal of Psychology*, 38: 503-10.
- Batlivala, S. (1990). *Stress: Your Friend or Foe?* Bombay: Wagle Process Studio and Press Pvt. Ltd.
- Beck, A. (1970). Cognitive therapy: The nature and relation to behaviour therapy. *Behaviour Therapy*, 1: 184-200.
- Bedian, A.G., & Armenokis, A.A. (1981). A path analytic

study of the consequences of role conflict and ambiguity. *Academy of Management Journal*, 24: 417-24.

- Beehr, T.A. (1976). Perceived situational moderators of the relationship between subjective role ambiguity and role strain. *Journal of Applied Psychology*, 61: 35-40.
- Beehr, T.A., (1984). Stress and coping research: Methodological issues. In A. S. Sethi & R.S. Schuler (Eds.), *Handbook of Organizational Stress Coping Strategies*. Cambridge, MA: Ballinger Publishing Company.
- ———— (1984). The themes of social psychological stress in work organisations: From roles to goals. Paper for the Seventh Annual Sympasia on Applied Behavioural Science, Virginia Polytechnic Institute and State University, Blochsburg, Virginia, Nov.
- ———— (1985a). Organizational stress and employees effectiveness: A job characteristics approach. In T.A. Beehr & R.S. Bhagat (Eds.), *Human Stress and Cognition in Organizations*. New York: John Wiley & Sons.
- Beehr, T.A, & Bhagat, R.S. (1985). Introduction to human stress and cognition in organisations. In T.A. Beehr & R.S. Bhagat (Eds.), *Human Stress and Cognition in Organizations*: An Integrated Perspective. New York: John Wiley & Sons.
- Beehr, T.A., & Franz, T.M., (1987). The current decade about the meaning of job stress. In J.M. Ivancevich & D.C. Ganster (Eds.), *Job Stress: From Theory to Suggestions*. New York: Haworth Press.
- Beehr, T.A., & Newman, J.E., (1978). Job stress, employee health, and organizational effectiveness: A facet analysis, model and literature review. *Personnel Psychology*, 31: 665-69.
- Beehr, T.A., Walsh, J.T., & Talur, T.D. (1976). Relationship of stress to individually and organizationally valued stress: Higher order needs as moderators. *Journal of Applied Psychology*. 61: 41-47.

- Bensahel, J. (1974). How to stay sane during a corporate crisis. *International Management.* 29: 17-18.
- Benson, H., (1975). *The Relaxation Response.* New York: Morrow.
- Berger, B.G., & Owen, D.R., (1983). Mood alteration with swimming: Swimmers really do "feel-better". *Psychosomatic Medicine.* 50: 418-33.
- Bhagat, R.S., Lindholm, H., Mc Quaid, S.J., & Segovis, J. (1985). Total life stress: A multi-method validation of construct and its effects on organizational valued outcomes and withdrawal behaviours'. *Journal of Applied Psychology.* 70: 202-14.
- Bhandarkar, A., & Singh, P. (1986). Managerial stress: A study of cyclical perspective. *Abhigyan,* Autumn, 7: 42.
- Boutcher, S.H., & Landers, D.M. (1988). The effect of vigorous exercise on anxiety, heart rate, and alpha activity of runners and non-runners. *Psychophysiologic,* 25: 696-702.
- Brief, A.P., Schuler, R.S., & Vansell, M. (1981). *Managing Stress.* Boston: Little Brown.
- Brief, A.R., & Aldag, R.J. (1976). Correlates of the role-stress Indices. *Journal of Applied Psychology.* 61: 468-72.
- Brook, A., (1973). Mental stress at work. *The Practitioner.* 210: 500-08.
- Brown, R.H., (1977). An evaluation of the effectiveness of relaxation training as a treatment modality for the hyperkinetic child (Doctoral dissertation, Texas Technological University). *Dissertation Abstracts International,* 38: 2847B.
- Buck, V.E., (1972). *Working Under Pressure.* London: Staples Press.
- Bunce, D., & West, M.A., (1996). Stress management and innovation interventions at work. *Human Relations.* 49: 209-31.
- Bures, Z., & Buresova, M., (1974). The operator in an

experimentally induced stress and his performance. *Studia Psychologica.* 16: 169-98.

- Cannon, W.B., (1914). The interrelations of emotions as suggested by recent physiological researches. *American Journal of Psychology.* 25: 256-82.
- Cannon, W.B., (1935). Stresses and strains of homeostasis. *American Journal of Medical Sciences.* 189: 1-14.
- Caplan, R.D., Cobb, S., & French, J.R.P. (1975). Relationships of cessation of smoking with job stress, personality, and social support. *Journal of Applied Psychology.* 60: 211-19.
- Caplan, R.D., (1972). Organizational stress and individual strain: A social psychological study of risk factors in coronary heart disease among administrators, engineers, and scientists. *Dissertation Abstracts International,* 32: (11B), 6706B.
- Caplan, R.D., & Jones, K.W., (1975). Effects of workload, role ambiguity, and type A Personality on anxiety, depression, and heart rate. *Journal of Applied Psychology.* 60: 713-19.
- Carrington, P. (1978), *Clinically Standardized Meditation Instructor's Kit.* Kendall Park N.J: Pace Educational Systems.
- Carver, C.S., Weintraub, J.K., & Scheier, M. F., Assessing coping strategies: A theoretically based approach. *Journal of Personality and Social Psychology.* 56: 267-83.
- Chase, D.J., (1972). Sources of mental stress and how to avoid them, *Supervisory Management.* 17: 23-26.
- Cherns, A., (1976). The principles of socio-technical design. *Human Relations.* 9: 783-92.
- Christopher, O., (1982). Type A personality as a moderator for the effect of role conflict, role ambiguity and role overload on individual strain. *Journal of Human Stress.* 8: 8-14.
- Cobb, S. & Rose, R.M., (1973). Hypertension, peptic

ulcer, and diabetes in air traffic controllers. *Journal of American Medical Association.* 224: 489-92.

- Cobb, S., (1971). The frequency of rheumatic disease. Cambridge: Harvard University Press.
- ——— (1974). A model for life events and their consequences. In B.S. Dohrenwend & B.P. Dohrenwend (Eds.), *Stressful life events: Their nature and effect.* New York: Wiley.
- Cobb, S., (1976). Social support as a moderator of life stress. *Psychosomatic Medicine.* 38: 5: 300-314.
- Cofer, C.N., & Appley, M.H. (1964). *Motivation: Theory and Research.* New York: Wiley.
- Cohen, F., & Lazarus, R.S., (1979). Coping with stresses of illness. In G.C. Stone, I. Cohen, & N.E. Adler (Eds.), *Health Psychology,* San Franisco: Jossey-Boss.
- Cohen, S., (1980). After effects of stress on human performance and social behaviour: A review of research and theory. *Psychological Bulletin.* 88: 82-108.
- Colligan, M.J., Smith, M.J., & Hurrell, J.J. (1977). Occupational incidence rate of mental health disorders. *Journal of Human Stress.* Sept, 34-39.
- Colquhoum, W.P., (1976). Accidents, injuries, and shift work. In P.G. Rentos & R.D. Shepard (Eds.), *Shift Work and Health.* Washington, D.C.: U.S. Govt. Printing Office.
- Conard, D.C., (1952). Toward a more productive concept of mental health. *Mental Hygiene.* 36: 456-66.
- Cooper, C.L., & Marshall, J., (1976). Occupational sources of stress: A review of the literature relating to coronary heart disease and mental ill health. *Journal of Occupational Psychology.* 49: 11-28.
- Cooper, C.L., (1984). *Psychological Stress and Cancer.* New York: John Wiley & Sons.
- ——— (1987). The experience and management of stress: job and organizational determinants. In A.W. Riley & S.J. Zaccaro (Eds.)., *Occupational Stress and Organizational Effectiveness.* New York: Praejer.
- Cooper, C.L., & Roden, J., (1985). Mental health and

satisfaction among the officers. *Social Science and Medicine*. 22: 588-92.

- Cox, T., (1978). *Stress*. London: MacMillon Press Ltd.
- Crain, R.D., (1974). The effect of work values on the relationship between job characteristics and job satisfaction. *Dissertation abstracts International*. 50: 243-48.
- Crouter, A.C., (1984). Spillover from family to work: The neglected side of the work-family interface: *Human relation*. 37: 425-42.
- Crown, S., & Gisp, A.H., (1966). A sort clinical diagnostic self-rating scale for psychoneurotic patients: The Middlesex Hospital Questionnaire. *British Journal of Psychiatry*. 112: 917-23.
- Crump, J.H., (1979). Review of stress in air traffic control: Its measurement and effects. *Aviation, Space, and Environmental Undecide*. 50: 243-48.
- David, C.A., (1991). The effect of the music and relaxation techniques in pain and anxiety of women gynaecological procedures. Unpublished Master's Thesis. Florida State University.
- Davidson, M.J., & Cooper, C.L., (1983). *Stress and Woman Manager*. Oxford: Martin Robertson Publishers.
- Davidson, P.O., & Davidson, S.M., (1980). *Behavioural Medicine: Changing Health Life Style*. New York: Brunner\Mazel.
- Davidson, R.J., & Schewartz, G.E., (1976). The psychology of relaxation and related states: A multi-process theory. In D.I. Mostefsky (Ed.), *Behaviour Control and Modification of Psychological Activity*. Englewood Cliffs: Prentice Hall.
- Davison, J.T.H., (1899). *Music and Medicine*. Lancet, 1159, 1160, 1162.
- DeVille, J., (1970). Coping with the pressures of your job. *Supervisory Management*. 15: 2-5.
- Dinning, W.D., & Crampton, J., (1989). The Krantz health opinion survey: Correlation with preventive

health behaviors and intensions. *Psychological Reports.* 64: 59-64.

- Dohrenwend, B.S., & Dohrenwend, B.P., (1974). *Stressful Life Events: Their Nature and Effects.* N.Y.: Wiley.
- Druker, P., (1954). *The Practice of Management.* New York: Harper & Row.
- Dunbar, H.F., (1947). *Mind and Body.* New York: Random House.
- Dynerman, S.B., & Hayes, O.L., (1991). The best jobs in America for parents who want careers and tennis for children too. New York: Rawson Associates.
- Eden, K., Sherom, A., Kellerman, J.J., Arouson, J., & French, J.R.P., 1977. Stress, anxiety and coronary risk in a supportive society. In C.D. Speilberger & I.G. Sarason (Eds.), *Stress and Anxiety,* (Vol. V): 251-67. N.Y.: Johns Wiley & Sons.
- Edmonston, W.E. Jr. (1981). *Hypnosis and Relaxation: Modern Verification of an old Equation.* New York: Wiley.
- Endler, N.S. (1975). A person-situation interaction model of anxiety.In C.D. Speilberger & I.G. Sarason (Eds.)., *Stress and Anxiety.* Vol. 1. Washington, DC: Hemisphere.
- ——— (1980). Personal-situation interaction and anxiety. In I.L. Katash & L.B. Schlesinger (Eds.), *Handbook on Stress and Anxiety: Contemporary Knowledge, Theory, and Treatment.* San Francisco: Jassey-Rass.
- Erikson, J., Edward, D., & Gundrson, E.K., (1973). Status congruency and mental health. *Psychological Reports.* 33: 395-401.
- Fair, E.W., (1976). Keeping pressures out of your working life. *Supervisor.* 38: 23-24.
- Fiedler, F.E., (1967). *A Theory of Leadership Effectiveness.* New York: McGraw-Hill.
- Fleishman, E.A., Hárris, F., & Burtt, N.E. (1955). *Leadership and Supervision in Industry.* Columbus: Ohio

State University.

- Folkman, S., & lazarus, R.S., (1980). An analysis of coping in middle aged community sample. *Journal of Health and Social Behaviour.* 21: 216-39.
- ——— (1985). If it changes it must be a process: Study of emotion and coping during three stages of a college examination. *Journal of Personality and Social Psychology.* 40: 140-70.
- Folkman, S., Lazarus R.S., Green, R.J., & Delongis, A. (1986). Appraisal, coping, health status, and psychological symptoms. *Journal of Personality and Social Psychology.* 50: 571-79.
- Folkman, S., Schaefer, C., & Lazarus, R.S. (1979). Cognitive processes as mediators of stress and coping. In V. Hamilton & D.M. Warburton (Eds.), *Human Stress and Cognition: An Information Processing Approach.* London: Wiley.
- Fowles, D.C. (1980). The three arousal model: Implications of Gray's two factor theory for heart rate, electrodermal activity, and psychopathy. *Psychophysiology.* 17: 87-104.
- Frank, J., (1961). *Persuation and Healing.* Johns Hopkins Press.
- Frankenhaeuser, M., & Gardell. B., (1976). Underload and overload in working life: Outline of a multidisciplinary approach. *Journal of Human Stress.* 2: 35-45.
- French, J.R.P. Jr, & Caplan, R.D., (1972). Occupational stress and individual strain. In Marrow, A.J. (Ed.), *The Failure of Success.* New York: Amacom.
- French, J.R.P. Jr., Rodgers. W., & Cobb. S., (1974). Adjustment as person-environment fit. In Coelho, G.V., Hamburg, D.A., & Adams, J.E. (Eds.), *Coping and Adaptation,* New York: Basic Books.
- Friedman, M., & Rosenman R., (1974). *Type A Behaviour and Your heart.* New York: Knoof.
- Furnham, A., & Schaeffer, R., (1984). Person-environment fit, job satisfaction and mental health.

Journal of Occupational Psychology. 57: 295-307.

- Galloway, D. (1984). Mental health, absence from work, stress and satisfaction in a sample of New Zealand primary school teachers. *Australia & New Zealand Journal of Psychiatry.* 18: 359-63.
- Gardel, B.V., (1975). Technology, alienation and mental health: Summary of a social psychological research programme on technology and the worker. Reports from the Department of Psychology. U. Stockholm, No. 456, 11.
- Gavin, J.F., & Axelrod, W.L., (1977). Managerial stress and strain in a mining organization. *Journal of Vocational Behaviour.*
- Gemmill, R., & Heisler, W.J. (1972). Machiavellianism as a factor in managerial job strain, job satisfaction, and upward mobility. *Academy of Management Journal.* 15: 51-62.
- Girodo, M., (1977). Self-talk: Mechanism in anxiety and stress management. In C.D. Spielberger, & I.G. Sarason (eds.), *Stress and Anxiety* (vol. 4). Washington, DC: Hemisphere.
- Glass, D.C., (1977). *Behaviour Patterns, Stress and Coronary Diseases.* Hillsdale, N.J.: Eribaum.
- Glass, D.C., & Singer., J.E., (1972). *Urban Stress.* New York: Academic Press.
- Goldberger, L., & Breznity, S., *Handbook of Stress: Theoretical and Clinical Aspects.* N. Y.: The Free Press.
- Goodstein, L.D. *The 1986 Annual: Developing Human Resources.* San Diego, California: University Associates, 121-33.
- Gore, S. (1973). The influence of social support and related variables in ameliorating the consequences of job loss. Unpublished Doctoral dissertation, University of Pennsylvania.
- ——— (1978). The effect of social support in moderating the health consequences of unemployment. *Journal of Health and Social Behaviour.* 19: 115-65.

- ——— (1987). 'Perspective on social support and research on stress moderating processes'. *Journal of Organizational Behaviour Management,* 8 (2): 87-103.
- Greenhaus, J.H., & Parasuraman, S., (1987). A work-non-work interactive perspective of stress and its consequences. In Ivancevich, J.M. & Ganster, D.C. (Eds.), *Job Stress: From Theory to Suggestion.* N.Y. The Haworth Press.
- Gupta, A., (1999). Moderating effect of job attribution on the relationship of role stress and job behaviour and health. Doctoral dissertation. Banaras Hindu University.
- Halim-Abel, & Ahmad, A., (1982). Social support and managerial effective responses to job stress. *Journal of Occupational Behaviour.* 3: 281-95.
- Hall, D.T., (1986). *Career Development in Organization.* San Francisco, CA: Jossey Bass.
- Hall, D.T., & Garden, F.E., (1973). Career choices of married women: Effects on conflict, role behaviour and satisfaction. *Journal of Applied Psychology.* 58: 42-48.
- Hall, D.T., & Lawler, E.E., (1971). Job pressure and research performance. *American Scientist.* 69: 64-73.
- ——— (1990). Job characteristics and pressures and the organizational integration of professionals. *Administrative Science Quarterly.* 15: 271-81.
- Hanmer, W.C., & Tosi, H.L., (1974). Relationship of role conflict and role ambiguity to job involvement measures. *Journal of Applied Psychology.* 59: 497-99.
- Hargopal, K., (1980). Role stress variables and company satisfaction and job involvement:: Personality factors as moderators. *Managerial Psychology.* 1: 13-25.
- Hargopal, K., & Ravi Kumar, R., (1979). Company satisfaction in relation to certain job attitudes and role stress variables. *Indian Journal of Applied Psychology.* 16: 61-67.
- Harrison, R.V., (1976). Job stress as person-environment misfit. A symposium presented at the 84th

Annual Convention of the American Psychological Association, Sept.

- Hart, J.D., (1982). Failure to complete treatment of or headache: A multiple regression analysis. *Journal of Counseling and Clinical Psychology.* 50: 781-82.
- Haward, J., (1978). Managing stress and job tension. The Labour Gazette. 78: 61-64.
- Haward, J.H., Rechnitzer, P.A., & Cunningham, D.A., (1975). Coping with job tension-effective and ineffective methods, *Public Personnel Management.* 4: 317-26.
- Hendrix, W.H., Ovalle, N.K., & Troxler, R.G., (1985). Behavioural and physiological consequences of stress and its antecedent factors. *Journal of Applied Psychology.* 70: 188-201.
- Hinkle, L.E., (1973). The concept of stress in biological and social sciences. *Science, Medicine and Man.* 1: 31-48.
- Hodges, D.A., (1980). *Handbook of Music Psychology.* Lawrence, K.S.: National Association for Music Therapy.
- Holmes, T.H., & Rahe, R.H., (1967). Social readjustment rating scale. *Journal of Psychosomatic Research.* 11: 213-18.
- House, B.H., & Rizzo, J.R., (1972). Role conflict and ambiguity as critical variables in a model of organizational behaviour. *Organizational Behaviour and Human Performance.* 7: 465-505.
- House, J.S., (1972). The relationship of intrinsic and extrinsic work motivations to occupational stress and coronary heart disease risk. Unpublished doctoral dissertation, University of Michigan.
- House, J.S., & Wells, J.A., (1977). Occupational stress, social support and health. Paper presented at conference on Reducing Occupational Stress, New York. In J. E. McGrath (Ed.), *Social and Psychological Factors in Stress*, Holt, N.Y: Rinehart, and Winston.
- House, J.S., Michael, A.J., Wells, J.A., Kaplan, B.H., & Landerman, L.R., (1979). Occupational stress and health among factory workers. *Journal of Health and*

Social Behaviour. 20: 139-160.

- Innes, J.M., & Adreinne, C., (1985). Job involvement as a moderator variable in the life events stress-illness relationship. *Journal of Occupational Behaviour.* 6: 299-303.
- Insel, P.M., & Moss, R.H., (1974). *Health and Social Environment.* Lexengton: D.C., Health & Company.
- Ivancevich, J.M., & Gonster, D.C., (1987). *Job Stress: From theory to Suggestional.* New York. The Haworth Press.
- Ivancevich, J.M., & Matteson, M.T., (1980). *Stress and Work: A Managerial Perspective.* Gleinview, IL: Scott Foresman.
- ——— (1981). *Stress and Work* . Glenview, J.L: Foreman Company.
- ——— (1987). Organizational level stress management interventions. In J.M. Ivancevich (Ed.). *Job Stress: From Theory to Suggestions.* New York. The Hawarth Press.
- ——— (1988). Promoting the individual's health and well-being, In C.L. Cooper & R. Payne (Eds.), *Causes, Coping and Consequences of Stress at Work.* London: John Wiley.
- Ivancevich, J.M., & Donnelly, H.H. (1975). Relation of organizational structure to job satisfaction, anxiety, and performance: Measures, research and contingencies. *Administrative Science Quarterly.* 20: 272-80.
- Jackson, S.E., (1984). 'Organizational practices for preventive born out'. In A.S. Sethi, & R.S. Schuler (eds.), *Handbook of Organizational Stress and Coping Strategies.* Cambridge. MA: Ballinger.
- Jagdish, (1983). An investigation into the relationship of perceived occupational stress with job satisfaction and mental health of first level supervisors. Doctoral dissertation. Banaras Hindu University.
- Jahoda, M., (1958). *Current Concepts of Positive Mental Health.* New York: Basic Books Inc., Publishers.

- Jamal, M., (1984). Job stress and job performance controversy: An empirical assessment. *Organizational Behaviour & Human Performance.* 32: 1-21.
- James, L.R., & Jones, A.P., (1976). Organizational structure: A review of structural dimension and their conceptual relationship with individuals attitudes and behaviour. *Organizational Behaviour and Human Performance.* 16: 74-113.
- Janis, I.L., Mohl, G.F., Kagon, J., & Holt, R.R., (1969). *Personality: Dynamics, Development and Assessment.* New York: Horcorest, Brace and Jovanovich, Ince.
- Jaremko, M.E., (1983). Stress inoculation training for social anxiety. In D. Meichenbaum, & M.E. Jaremko (Eds.), *Stress Reduction and Prevention.* New York: Plenum Press.
- Jette, M., (1984). Stress coping through physical activity, In A.S. Sethi & R.S. Schuler (Eds.), *Handbook of Organizational Stress and Coping Strategies.* Cambridge, MA: Ballinger.
- Jick, T.D., (1985). As the falls: budget cuts and the experience of stress in organisations, In T.A. Beehr & R.S. Bhagat (Eds.), *Human Stress and Cognition in Organizations.* New York: John Wiley.
- Johnson, J.H. & Sorason, I.G., (1979). Recent developments in research in life stress. In V. Hamilton & D.M. Warburton (Eds.), *Human Stress and Cognition.* New York: Wiley.
- Johnson, L.Y., (1981). The pineal gland as a modulator of the adrenal and thyroid axes. In R.J. Reiste (Ed.), *The Pineal gland, Extra-reproductive effects.* Vol. III. Boca-Raton: CRC Press, 107-152.
- Jourard, S.M., (1971). *Self-disclosure: An experimental analysis of the transparent self.* New York: Wiley.
- Julius. S., (1984). Implications for hypertension. In N.I.H. stress reactivity and cardiovascular disease: Proceedings of the working conference (pp. 63-71), Washington, D.C. Department of Health and Human Services.

- Kagan, N.I., Kagan, H., & Watson, M.G., (1994). Stress reduction in workplace: The effectiveness of psycho-educational programmes. *Journal of Counseling Psychology.* 42: 71-78.
- Kahn, R.L., (1973) Conflict ambiguity and overload: Three elements in job stress. *Occupational and Mental Health.* 3: 2-9.
- Kahn, R.L., & Quinn, R.P., (1970). Role stress: A framework for analysis. In A. McLean (Ed.), *Mental Health and Work Organization.* Chicago: Rand McNally.
- Kahn, R.L., Wolfe, D.M., Quinn, R.R., Sonek, J.D., & Rosenthal, R.A., (1964). *Organizational Stress: Studies in Role Conflict and Ambiguity.* New York: Wiley.
- Karcher, C.J., & Leviden, L.L., (1982). Is work conduction to self-destruction? *Suicide and Life Threatening Behaviour.* 12: 151-57.
- Katz, D., & Kahn, D., (1966). *The Social Psychology of Organizations.* New York: Wiley.
- Katz, R., (1985). Organizational stress and early socialization experiences. In T.A. Beehr & R.S. Bhagat (Eds.), *Human Stress and Cognition in Organizations.* New York: John Wiley.
- Kaye, B.L., (1982), *Up is Not the Only Way.* Englewood Cliffs, N J: Prentice Hall.
- Kearns, J.L., (1973). *Stress Industry.* London: Priory Press.
- Keller, R.T., (1981). Job stress and employees performance in a manufacturing plant. Paper presented at a meeting of the National Academy of Management, San. Diego.
- Kendall, P.C., & Bennis, K.M., (1983). Thought and action in psychotherapy: The cognitive-behavioural approaches, In Hersen, A.E. Kazdin & A. S. Bellack (Eds.), *The Clinical Psychology Handbook.* New York: Pergamon Press.
- Ketz de Vries, M.F.R., (1984). 'Organizational stress management audit: In A.S. Sethi & R.S. Schuler (Eds.),

Handbook of Organizational Stress and Coping Strategies. Cambridge, MA: Ballinger.

- Kimball, W.H., (1979). Psychological correlates of tension headaches. *Dissertation Abstracts International.* 39 (10B): 5073B.
- Kisch, E.S., (1985). Stressful events and onset of diabetes mellitus. *Israeli Journal of Medical Sciences.* 21: 256-58.
- Kobasa, S.C., (1982). Commitment and coping in stress resistance among lawyers. *Journal of Personality and Social Psychology.* 41: 707-14.
- Kopleman, R.E., (1986). *Managing Productivity in Organization.* New York: McGraw-Hill.
- Kornhauser, A., (1965). *Mental Health of Industrial Worker.* New York: Wiley.
- Lai, G., (1995). Work and family roles and psychological well being in urban China. *Journal of Health and Social Behaviour.* 36: 11-37.
- Landy, F.J., & Trumbo, D.A., (1976). *Psychology of Work Behaviour* . Homewood: De Dorsey Press.
- LaRocco, J.M., & Jones, A.P., (1978). Co-workers and labour support as moderators of stress-strain relationship in work situation. *Journal of Applied Psychology.* 63: 629-34.
- Latack, J.C., (1984). Career transition within organizations: An exploratory study of work, non-work and coping strategies. *Organizational Behavior and Human Performance.* 34: 296-322.
- Latak, J.C., (1986). Coping with job stress: Measures and future directions for scale development. *Journal of Applied Psychology.* 71: 377-85.
- Lawler, E.E., (1994). From job-based to competence-based organisations. *Journal of Organizational Behaviour.* 15: 3-15.
- Lazarus, R.S., (1966). *Psychological Stress and the Coping Process.* New York: McGraw Hill.
- Lazarus, R.S., (1975). A cognitively oriented

psychologist looks at biofeedback. *American Psychologist.* 30: 553-61.

- ———— (1980). The stress and coping paradigm. In C. Eisdorfeer, D. Cohen. & A. Kteiuwan (Eds.), *Theoretical Based for Psychopathology.* N.Y.: Spectrum.
- Lazarus, R.S., & Folkman, S., (1984). Coping and adaptation. In W.D. Certry (Ed.). *Handbook of Behavioural Medicine,* 282-325. N. Y.: Guilford.
- ———— (1984). *Stress, Appraisal, and Coping.* New York: Springer.
- Lazarus, R.S., & Cohen, J.B., (1976). Theory and method in the study of stress and coping in ageing individuals. 5th WHO Conference on Society; Stress and Disease. Stockholm, Sweden.
- Lazarus, R.S., & Launier, R., (1978). Stress-related transactions between person and environment. In L.A. Pervin & M. Lewis (Eds.), *Perspectives International Psychology.* New York: Plenum Press.
- Lefcourt, H.M., (1976). *Locus of Control: Current Trends in Theory and Research.* New York: Halstead.
- Lewin, K., (1951). *Field Theory in Social Science.* New York: Parker.
- Lewis, C.E., Biglan, A., & Steinbock, E., (1978). Self administered relaxation training and money deposit in the treatment of recurrent anxiety. *Journal Counseling and Clinical Psychology.* 46: 1274-83.
- Lewy, A.J., Wehr, T.A., Gold, P., & Goodwin, F.K., (1979). Plasma melatonin in manic depressive illness. In E. Nsden, I.J. Kopin, & B.J. Barchas (Eds.), *Catecholamines: Basic and Clinical Front-Liners,* (Vol.2). 1173-75.
- Lieberman, M.A., (1982). The effect of social support on response to stress. In Leo Goldman & S. Breznitz (Eds.), *Handbook of Stress: Theoretical & Clinical Aspects.* 764-80. N.Y.: Free Press.
- Lifcourt, H.M., (1984). New directions in research with the LOC construct. *Psychological Studies.* 29: 107-11.

- Likert, R., (1961). Measuring organizational performance. In E.A. Fleishman, (Ed.). *Studies in Personnel and Industrial Psychology.* Homewood. Illinois: Dorsey, 453-68.
- Little, P.A., (1986). Effect of stressful movie and music on physiological and affect arousal as a function of sensation seeking trait. *Dissertation Abstracts International,* 47, 3962 B.
- Locke, E.A., & Latham, G.D., (1984). *Goal Setting: A Motivational Technique That Works.* Englewood Cliff, N.J.: Prentice Hall.
- Lodahl, T.M., & Kejner, M., (1965). The definition and measurement of job involvement. *Journal of Applied Psychology.* 49: 24-33.
- London, M., & Klimoski, R.J., (1975). Self-esteem and job complexity as moderators of performance and satisfaction. *Journal of Vocational Behaviour.* 6: 293-304.
- Mack, D.A., Nelson, D.L., & Quick, J.C., (1998). The stress of organizational change: A dynamic process model. *Applied Psychology: International Review.* 47: 219-32.
- Maddi, S.R., & Kobasa, S.C., (1984). *The Hardy Executives: Health Under Stress.* Homewood, IL: Do Jones Irwin.
- Madhu, K., & Hargopal, K., (1980). Role conflict and role ambiguity in relation to job, job involvement, job performance, age and job tenure. *Indian Journal of Applied Psychology.* 17: 1-6.
- Margolis, B.L., Kores, W.H., & Quinn, R.P. (1974). Job stress: An unlisted occupational hazard. *Journal of Occupational Medicine.* 16: 654-61.
- Marks, C., & Banak, A., (1977). Help Yourself to health. *The Canadian Banker and the Institute of Canadian Banking Review.* 84: 48-50.
- Maranto, C.D., (1989b). The use of music therapy in the treatment of performance anxiety in musicians. Paper presented at the IV International Music Medicine

2222 Symposieem, Rancho Mirage, C.A.

- ——— (1992). The use of music therapy in the treatment of performance anxiety in musicians. In R. Spintage & R. Droh (Eds.), *Music and Medicine*. St. Louis: M.M.B. Music.
- Martin, J.E., Dubbert, P.M., & Cushman, W.C., (1990). Controlled trial of aerobic exercise in hypertension. *Circulation*. 81: 1560-67.
- Martin, N., (1984). Role stress and inability of leave as predictors of mental health. *Human Relations*. 37: 969-83.
- Maslach, C., & Jackson, S.E., (1981). The measurement of experienced burnout. *Journal of Occupational Behavior*. 2: 99-113.
- Maslow, A.H., & Mittelman, E., (1951). *Principles of Abnormal Psychology*, New York: Harper and Bros.
- Mason, J.L., (1980). *Guide to Stress Reduction*. Culver City, CA: Peace Press.
- Mathney, K.B., Aycock, D.W., Pugh, J.L., Curlette, W.L., & Cannella, K.A., (1986). 'Stress coping: A qualitative and quantitative synthesis with implications for treatment'. *The Counseling Psychologist*. 14: 499-549.
- Matteson, M.T., & Ivancevich, J.M., (1987). *Controlling Work Stress: Effective Resources and Management Strategies*. San Francisco, CA: Jossey-Bass.
- McCubbin, J.A., Surwit, R.S., & Williams, R.B., (1985). Endogeneous opiate petides stress reactivity and risk for hypertension. *Hypertension*. 7: 808-17.
- McGrath, J.E., (1976). Stress and behaviour in organizations. In M.D. Dunnette (Ed.), *Handbook of Industrial and Organizational Psychology*, Chicago: Rand McNally.
- Meglino, B.M., (1977). Stress and performance: Are they always incompatible? *Supervisory Management*. 22: 2-12.
- Meichenbaum, D. (1975). Self-instructional methods. In F.H. Kanfer & A.P. Goldstein (Eds.), *Helping People*

Change. New York: Pergamon Press.

- ——— (1977). *Cognitive Behaviour Modification: An Integrated Approach*. New York: Plenum.
- Meredith, I.T., Jennings, G.L., Esler, M.D., Dewar, E.M., Bruce, A.M., Fario, V.A., & Korner, P.I., (1990). Time course of the antihypertensive and autonomic effects of regular endurance exercise in human subjects. *Journal of Hypertension*. 8: 859-66.
- Metzler, R., & Bermans, T., (1991). The effect of sedative music on anxiety and branchoscopy patients. In C.D. Marants (Ed.), *Application of Trunsic in Medicine*, Washington DC: National Association for Music Therapy.
- Meyer, A., (1958). *Psychobiology: A Science of Man*, translated by E.F. Winter, & A.M. Basser. Springfield, III; Charles Themes.
- Milsum, J.H., (1984). *Health, Stress and Illness: A Systems Approach*. New York: Praeger Publications.
- Morris, J.H., & Koch, J.L., (1979). Impact of role perceptions on organizational commitment, job involvement, and psychosomatic illness among three vocational groupings. *Journal of Vocational Behaviour*. 14: 88-101.
- Morris, J.H., & Snyderman, R.A., (1979). A second look at n-Ach and autonomy as moderator of role perception outcome relationship. *Journal of Applied Psychology*. 64: 173-78.
- Moss, L., (1981). *Management of Stress*. Ontario: Addison-Wesley.
- Mott, P.E., (1976). Social and psychological adjustment to shift work. In P.G. Pentoś & R.D. Shepard (Eds.), *Shift Work and Health*. Washington, DC: U.S. Govt. Printing Office.
- Mott, P.I., (1972). *The Characteristics of Effective Organisations*. New York: Harper & Raw.
- Murphy, L.R., (1984). Occupational stress management: A review and appraisal. *Journal of Occupational Psychology*. 57: 367-72.

- ——— (1984b). Stress management in highway maintenance workers. *Journal of Occupational Medicine.* 26: 436-42.
- ——— (1985). Individual coping strategies. In C.L. Cooper & M.J. Smith (Eds.), *Job Stress and Blue Collar Workers,* New York. John Wiley.
- ——— (1988). Work place interventions for stress reduction and prevention. In C.L. Cooper & R. Paye (Eds.), *Causes, Coping and Consequences of Stress of Work,* Wiley, Chichestic.
- Neves, I.F., (1969). Social adaptation and accidents on job. *Revista Interamericca de Psicologia.* 3: 139-62.
- Newton, T.J., (1992). Stress management in caring services. In C. Duncan (Ed.). *The Evaluation of Public Management: Concepts and Techniques for the 1990s.* Basingstoke, Macmillan.
- Newton, T.J., & Keenan, A., (1985). Coping with work related stress. *Human Relations.* 38: 107-26.
- Ostberg, O., & Nelson C., (1985). Emergency technology and stress. In C.L. Cooper & M.J. Smith (Eds.). *Job Stress and Blue Collar Workers.* New York: John Wiley.
- Overbeke, J.E., (1975). Pressures built on today's managers, *Industry Week.* 187: 21-24.
- Paine, W.S., (1982). *Job Stress and Burnout: Research, Theory and Intervention.* London: Sage Publication.
- Pandey, N., & Naidu, R.K., (1986). Effort and outcome orientations as moderators of stress-strain relationship. *Psychological Studies.* 31: 207-14.
- Parasuraman, S., & Alutto, J.A., (1981). An examination of the organizational antecedents of stressors at work. *Academy of Management Journal.* 24: 48-67.
- Pareek, U., (1981). *Organizational Role Stress: Manual.* Ahmedabad: Navin Publications.
- ——— (1982). Executive glow up and burnout. Summary of L & T lectures delivered on Feb. 20, 1982, Ahmedabad: Indian Institute of Management.
- ——— (1983b). Preventing and resolving conflict. In

L.D. Goodstein & J.W. Pfeiffer (Eds.), *The* 1983 *Annual for Facilitators, Trainers, and Consultants.* 115-118. San Deigo, California: University Associates.

- Pareek, U., (1986). Developing and increasing role efficacy. In J.W. Pfeiffer,& Pareek, U. (Eds.), *Motivating Organizational Roles: Role Efficacy Approach.* Jaipur: Rawat Publications.
- ——— (1987b). *Moviating Organizational Roles: Role Efficacy Approach.* Jaipur: Rawat Publications.
- ———— (1993). *Making Organizational Roles Effective.* New Delhi: Tata McGraw-Hill Publishing Co. Ltd.
- Patel, C., (1993). Yoga-based therapy. In P.M. Lehrer & R.L. Woolfolk. *Principles and Practice of Stress Management.* New York. Guilford Press.
- Payne, R., (1980). 'Organizational stress and support.' In C.L. Cooper & R. Payne (Eds.), *Current Concerns in Occupational Stress.* New York: John Wiley.
- Pearlin, L.I., & Schooler, C., (1978). The structure of coping. *Journal of Health and Social Behaviour.* 19: 3-21.
- Perronet, F., Massicotte, D., Paquee, J.E., Brisson, G., & de Champlain, J., (1989). Blood pressure and catecholamine responses to various challenges during exercise-recovery in man. *European Journal of Applied Psychology.* 58: 551-55.
- Pestonjee, D.M., (1989). Role stress in government administration: Suggested HRD interventions. Paper presented at Second National Conference of HRD Network, Delhi.
- Pestonjee, D.M., (1992). *Stress and Coping.* New Delhi: Sage Publications India Ltd.
- Pestonjee, D.M., & Singh, G.P., (1987). Organizational behaviour issues for managers and system analysts. Working Paper. Indian Institute of Management, Ahmedabad.
- ———— (1988). Does Type-A behaviour moderate the stress-anger relationship in case of managers. Working Paper No. 743, Indian Institute of Management,

Ahmedabad.

- Pestonjee, D.M., & Singh. U.B., (1981). Locus of control as a moderator of role stress-job satisfaction relationship, working Paper No. 402. Indian Insti.ute of Management, Ahmedabad.
- Pierce, J.L., & Newstrom, J.W., (1983). 'The design, flexible work schedules and employee responses: relationships and process.' *Journal of Occupational Behaviour,* 4: 247-62.
- Pillai, V.K., (1987). A diagnosis of police stress: A case study of Ahmedabad city Police. A paper presented at the XX All India Police Service Congress.
- Pines, A.M., & Aronson, E., (1981). *Burnout: From Tedium to Personal Growth.* New York: Free Press.
- Pinneau, S.R. Jr., (1975). Effect of social support on psychological and physiological strains. Unpublished doctoral dissertation. University of Michiton. Dissertation Abstracts International. 36: 5359-B.
- ——— (1976). Effect of social support on occupational stress and strain. 84th Annual Convention of American Psychological Association (Sept).
- Powell, L.H., (1984). Can the Type A Behaviour pattern be altered myocordial infraction. *Psychosomatic Medicine.*
- Quick, J.C., & Quick, J.D., (1979). Reducing stress through preventive management. *Human Resource Management.* Fall. 15-22.
- Quinn, R.P., Seashore, S., & Mangione, I. (1971). *Survey of working conditions.* U.S. Government Printing Office.
- Rabkin, J.C., & Struening, E.L., (1976). Life events, stress and illness. *Science.* 194: 1013-20.
- Rahe, R.H., (1968). Life change measurement as a predictor of illness. In Proceedings of the Royal Society of Medicine. 61: 1124-26.
- Rahe, R.H., Meyer, M., Smith, M., Kjaerg, G., & Holmes, T.H., (1964). Social stress and illness onset. *Journal of Psychosomatic Research.* 8: 35-44.

- Ramchandra Rao, S.K., (1983b). The conception of stress in Indian thought: The practical involvement in Gita and Ayurveda. *NIMHANS Journal.* 1: 123-31.
- Ramchandran, G., (1989). Can't we reduce stress factors on the police: Administrative Issues. SPIPA, Ahmedabad.
- Revicki, D.A., & May, H. Jr., (1985). Occupational stress, social support, and depressions. *Health Psychology.* 4: 61-77.
- Rizoo, J.R., House, R.J., & Lirtzman, S.I., (1970). Role conflict and ambiguity in complex organizations. *Administrative Science Quarterly.* 15: 150-63.
- Roskies, E., (1983). Stress management for Type A individuals. In D. Meichenbaum & M. Jaremko (Eds.), *Stress Prevention and Management: a Cognitive Behavioural Approach.*
- Ross, R.R., & Altmair, E.M., (1994). *Interventions in Occupational Stress.* Sage: New York.
- Roth, D.L., & Holmes, D.S., (1987). Influence of aerobic-exercise training and relaxation training on physical and psychologic health following stressful life events. *Psychosomatic Medicine.* 49: 355-65.
- Sales, S.M., & House, J., (1971). Job dissatisfaction as a possible risk factor in coronary heart disease. *Journal of Chronic Diseases.* 23: 861-73.
- Sandler, I., Ruse, F., Specer, L., & Harpen, P., (1983). Person-environment interaction and locus of control: Laboratory, therapy and classroom studies. In H.M. Lefcourt (Ed.), *Research With the Locus of Control.* New York: Academic Press.
- Sarason, I.G., & Johnson, J.H. (1979). Life stress, organizational stress, and goal satisfaction. *Psychological Reports.* 44: 75-79.
- Schawartz, G, Davidson, R., & Goleman, D., (1978). Patterning of cognitive and somatic processes in the self-regulation of anxiety: Effect of meditation verses exercise. *Psychosomatic Medicine.* 40: 321-28.
- Schuler, R.S., (1977). Role conflict and ambiguity as a

function of the task-structure-technology interaction. *Organizational Behaviour and Human Performance.* 20: 60-74.

- ———— (1977a). The effect of role perception on employees' satisfaction and performance moderated by employee ability. *Organizational Behaviour and Human Performance.* 18: 98-107.
- ———— (1980). 'Definition and conceptualization of stress in organizations, *Organizational Behaviour and Human Performance.* 24: 115-30.
- ———— (1984). Organizational stress and coping: a model and overview. In A.S.Sethi & Schuler, R.S. (Eds.), *Handbook of Organizational Stress and Coping Strategies.* Cambridge, M.A.: Ballinger.
- Schuler, R.S., & Sethi, A.S., (1984). Time management and leader communication behaviour. In A.S. Sethi & R.S. Schuler (Eds.), *Handbook of Organizational Stress and Coping Strategies.* Cambridge, MA: Ballinger.
- Schultz, D., (1977). *Growth Psychology: Models of Health Personality.* Van Nostrand: Reinhold.
- Schultz, J.H., (1932). Das autogene training. Konzentrative Selbstenspannung. Leipzig: Thieme.
- Schur, J.M., (1986). Alleviating behavioural stress with music-blow breathing in children undergoing bone marrow operations and lumber punctures. *Dissertation Abstracts International,* 48.
- Scott, W.E., (1966). Activation theory and task design. *Organizational Behaviour and Human Performance,* 1, 3-30.
- Selye, (1983). The stress concept: past, present and future. In C.L. Cooper (Ed.), *Stress Research: Issues for Eighties.* Chiester: Wiley.
- Selye, H., (1956). *The Stress of Life.* New York: McGraw Hill.
- ———— (1980). The stress concept today. In I.L., Kutash & L.B. Schteinger (Eds.), *Handbook cf Stress and Anxiety.* San Francisco: Jossey Bass.

• Sharma, B.R., & Sundarajan, P.S., (1983). Organizational determinants of labour management relations in India. *Indian Journal of Industrial Relations.* 19: 1-20.

• Sherom, A., Eden, D., Siberwasser, S. & Kellerman, J. J., (1973). 'Stresses and risk factors in coronary heart disease among occupational categories in Kibbutzin. *Social Science and Medicine.* 7: 875-92.

• Siddhantalankar, S., & Taraporewala, S.J., (1969). *Heritage of Vedic Culture.* Bombay: Taraporewala.

• Singh, B.K., (1988). Relationship of participation and alienation with job involvement. *Indian Journal of Industrial Relations.* 23: 498-507.

• Singh, G.P., (1987). Organizational climate as moderator of role stress-job satisfaction relationship for computer professionals. Ph.D. Dissertation, Gujarat University, Ahmedabad.

• Singh, M.P., (1989). A study of values and style of coping as related to outcome variables in public and private enterprises. Unpublished doctoral dissertation. Banaras Hindu University.

• Smit, M.J., Colligon, M., & Hurrell, J.J., (1980). A review of psychological stress research carried out by NIOSH, 1971 to 1976. In R.M. Selwatz (Ed.). *New Developments in Occupational Stress.* Cincinnate National Institute for Occupational Safety and Health.

• Spanos, N.P., Ollerhead, V.G., & Guynn, M.I., (1985-86). The effect of the instrumental treatments on pain magnitude and tolerance. Implications for theories of hypnotic analgesia. *Imagination, Cognition, and Personality.* 5: 321-37.

• Speilberger, C.D., (1979). *Understanding Stress and Anxiety.* New York: Harper & Row.

• Srivastava, A.K., & Krishna, A. (1991). Development of a functional role stress scale. *Advances in Psychology.* 6: 11-17.

• ———— (1989). Buffering effect of job satisfaction on job stress-strain relationship. *Advances in*

Psychology. 4: 89-95.

- Srivastava, A.K., & Krishna, A., (1992). Moderating effect of locus of control on relationship of occupational stress and job tension. *Journal of Psychological Researches*. 36: 53-58.
- Srivastava, A.K. & Veena (1999). A study of moderating effect of personality traits on the relationship between occupational stress and job and health strain. (In Press).
- Srivastava, A.K. (1983). Role-based stress and mental health of white collar employees. *Indian Journal of Clinical Psychology*. 10: 343-47.
- ——— (1985). Moderating effect of n-Ach on role stress job anxiety relationship. *Psychological Studies*. 30: 8-14.
- ——— (1990). Moderating effect of job attitudes on occupational stress-mental health relationship. *Indian Journal of Applied Psychology*. 27: 98-102.
- ——— (1997). Self-management of occupational stress: A cognitive-behavioural approach. *Indian Journal of Industrial Relations*. 32: 487-95.
- ——— (1997). Stress-resistant cognitive-behavioural patterns scale. (In Press).
- Srivastava, A.K., & Singh, H.S., (1988). Modifying effects of coping strategies on the relation of organizational role stress and mental health. *Psychological Reports*. 62: 1007-1009.
- Srivastava, A.K., & Singh, A.P., (1981). Construction and standardization of an occupational stress index: A pilot study. *Indian Journal of Clinical Psychology*. 8: 133-36.
- Srivastava, A.K., & Sinha, M.M., (1983). Perceived role stress as a function of ego-strength and job involvement of managerial personnel. *Psychological Studies*. 28: 8-12.
- Srivastava, O.N., & Bhatt, V.K., (1971). Middlesex hospital questionnaire Standardization of Hindi Version. *Indian Journal of Psychiatry*. 16: 283-86.

- Srivastava, U., (1997). Role of behavioural pattern and social support in stress-health relationship among managerial personnel. Unpublished Ph.D. dissertation, Banaras Hindu University, Varanasi.
- Stout, J.K., (1984). Supervisor's structuring and consideration behaviours and worker's job satisfaction, stress and health problems. *Rehabilitation Counseling Bulletin.* 28: 133-38.
- Student, K.R., (1975). Coping with psychological responsibility. *The Conference Board Record.* 12: 61-64.
- ———— (1977). Changing values and management stress. *Personnel Psychology.* 54: 48-55.
- Suinn, R.M., (1982). Interventions with Type A Behaviors. *Journal of Counseling and Clinical Psychology.* 6: 933-49.
- Symonds, Sir C.P., (1974). Use and abuse of the term flying stress. In Air Ministry, Psychological Disorders in Flying Personnel of Royal Air Force. H.M.S.D., London.
- Syrotuik, J.M., & Arey, C., (1982). Occupational stress, locus of control and health among men in a prairic province. *Canadian Journal of Behavioural Science.* 14: 122-33.
- Tache, J., Selye, H., & Day, S.B., (1979). *Cancer, Stress and Death.* New York: Plenum Medical Book Company.
- Tamarkin, L., Almeida, O.F., & Danforth, D.N., (1985). Melatonin and malignant disease photo-periodism, melatosin and the pineal. *Cebasym.* 117: 284-94.
- Thaut, M.H., (1989a). Physiological responses to music stimuli. In R.Unkefer (Ed.), *Music Therapy in the Treatment of Adults with Mental Disorders.* New York: Schirmer Books.
- Tiwari, G., (1986). Interpersonal trust as a moderator of stress-strain relationship. Paper presented at the U.G.C. National Seminar on the Role of Psychologists in H.R.D., University of Allahabad.
- Tosi, H., & Tosi., D., (1970). Some correlates of role conflict and ambiguity among public school teachers.

Journal of Human Relations. 18: 1063-75.

- Uris, A., (1972). How managers ease job pressures. *International Management.* 27: 45-46.
- Valecha, G.K., (1980). Construction of a new personality scale: Internal-external locus of control. *Bombay Psychologist.* 2: 27.
- Vincent, S., & Thompson, J.H., (1979a). Effect of music and biofeedback on alpha brain wave rhythms and attentiveness. *Journal of Research in Music Education.* 23: 3-18.
- Waldron, J., (1978). The Coronary prone behaviour pattern, blood pressure, employment, and socio-economic status in women. *Journal of Psychosomatic Research.* 22: 79-87.
- Wall, I.D., & Clegg, C.W., (1981). A longitudinal study of group work redesign. *Journal of Occupational Behaviour.* 2: 31-49.
- Wallace, P.K., & Benson, H., (1972). The Physiology of Meditation. *Scientific American.* 226: 84-90.
- Walsh, R.J., (1975). You can deal with stress. *Supervisory Management.* 20: 16-21.
- Weitz, J., (1970). Psychological research needs on the problems of human stress. In J.E., McGrath (Ed.). *Social and Psychological Factors in Stress.* N.Y: Holt, Rinehart and Winstein.
- Wells, J.A., (1984). The role of social support groups in stress coping in organizational settings. In A.S. Sethi & R.S. Schuler (Eds.), *Handbook of Organizational Stress and Coping Strategies.* Cambridge, M.A.: Ballinger.
- Wingate, P., (1972). *The Penguin Medical Encyclopaedia.* Middlesex: Penguin Books, Harmondsworth.
- Woffort, J.C., & Daly, P.S., (1997). A cognitive-affective approach to understanding in individual differences in stress propensity and resultant strain. *Journal of Occupational Health Psychology.* 2: 134-47.
- Wolff, H.G., (1950). Life stress and bodily disease—a formulation in life stress and bodily diseases:

Proceedings of Association for Research in Nervous and Mental Disorders, Dec. 2 & 3, 1949. New York, Baltimore: Williams & Wilkins.

- Wolshok, M.L., (1981). *Blue Collar Women: Pioneer on the Male Frontier.* New York: Anchor.
- Yadav, J.N., (1996). Effectiveness of confrontational writing technique in alleviating job stress and consequent strain. Doctoral dissertation, Banaras Hindu University.
- Yerks, R., & Dodson, J.D., (1908). The relationship of stimulus to rapidity of habit formation. *Journal of Comparative Neurological Psychology.* 18: 459-72.
- Zegans, L.S., (1982). Stress and development of somatic disorders. In L. Goldberger & S. Breznitz (Eds.), *Handbook of Stress. Theoretical and Clinical Aspects.* New York: The Free Press.

INDEX